2020
SEPTEMBER–DECEMBER

D1476680

m
mettle

BIBLE READING NOTES

TO INSPIRE
COURAGE
SPIRIT
CHARACTER

YOUTH FOR CHRIST

CWR

MIX
Paper from responsible sources
FSC® C015900

CONTENTS

Welcome to

mettle
COURAGE SPIRIT CHARACTER...

Welcome to what is sadly going to be the last issue of *Mettle* as we know it! We are no longer able to provide you with printed notes, but do check out the CWR website for updates as to how you might be able to access some *Mettle* content in other ways.

We draw this era to a close by looking at Discipleship (what it really means to follow Jesus and live for Him); Peer Pressure, and how we can use our influence for good; Humour, and how God actually has tons of it; and Obedience – not a particularly popular concept these days, but vital for demonstrating our trust in Jesus.

Do stay in touch (mettle@cwr.org.uk) and let us know how we can help you to carry on reading God's Word. We hope and pray you continue to seek God's best for your life, and talk to Him every day. Bye for now, and God bless!

The *Mettle* Team

TUES 1 SEP

DISCIPLESHIP

The maker

READ: 1 CORINTHIANS 2:10–16

KEY VERSE V16
'But we have the mind of Christ.'

Welcome to the core topic of this issue of *Mettle* – discipleship. Being a disciple means trying to follow someone's example. But who's the best person to follow? And why should you follow them? How do you decide? We're going to try to answer these very valid questions over the next couple of months.

First, an anecdote… There was a scientist who had a very good model of the solar system on her desk; completely to scale, it showed all the planets circling the sun. A friend, who didn't believe in God, saw it and asked the scientist who had made it, because he wanted to get one. The scientist saw an opportunity

and replied, 'What do you mean: "Who made it?" What a silly question! Nobody made it, it just appeared.' Her friend was not impressed: 'Just tell me who made it! Things like that don't just appear! Someone must have made it.' The scientist looked at her friend and smiled: 'You're right, somebody did make it. But here's the thing: you refuse to believe that this model just happened without a maker, so why do you believe that the real universe could exist without a creator?'

Do you want to follow Jesus but aren't quite sure what that means? Jesus encouraged people to ask questions so that they could discover more about God. Be confident that you were created for a reason and that Jesus wants you to follow His example. Over the next two weeks we will be looking at six key characteristics of being a disciple, learning some top discipleship tips and looking at what it means to be one of Jesus' disciples in today's world.

Pray

Father, thank You for creating the universe and for making me. Help me to understand more about You and to be willing to take opportunities to talk to others about You. Amen.

5

Believer

READ: PROVERBS 3:4–6

KEY VERSE V5
'Trust in the LORD with all your heart and lean not on your own understanding;'

The dictionary defines a disciple as somebody who believes in and follows the teachings of a leader, a philosophy or a religion.

Hidden within the word search below are six words that describe a disciple. Over the next few days we'll be unpacking what those words means together.

The word for today is **Believer**. Have you ever stopped and asked yourself what you believe? What or who you trust in?

Jesus said in John 12:46: 'I have come into the world as a light, so that no one who believes in me should stay in darkness.'

Sometimes we might feel in the dark about a lot of things but Jesus has promised to bring light and understanding when we believe in Him.

Discipleship Tip: Believe and trust in Jesus with all your heart.

⚭ *Think*

Who do you turn to for advice? Are you confident in trusting Jesus? Why not talk to Him about something that is puzzling you at the moment.

CORE THEME | DISCIPLESHIP 1

Follower

READ: MATTHEW 16:24–27

KEY VERSE V24
'Whoever wants to be my disciple must deny themselves and... follow me.'

The word for today is **Follower**. For you to be a disciple of Jesus you need to give yourself to God. As we grow in our love for Him, everything we have can be offered in service to Him – our money, our time, our home, our job, our thoughts, our moods, our love and our ambitions.

This can be really hard to understand and sometimes most of us struggle with the idea that, as a follower of Christ, we could be asked to offer everything we have to God in order that others would learn about Him and His love. But let's be comforted by the fact that everything we have comes from Him and He will always look after us. He will never ask for more than He knows we are able to give. On top of that, Jesus promised: 'Give, and it will be given to you' (Luke 6:38). Often we discover that, when we give our money, time or plans to God, He honours that self-sacrifice by blessing us in ways we can't imagine.

Discipleship Tip: Be willing to offer your all to God so that He can do amazing things in and through your life!

✚ *Challenge*

Read the list in the first paragraph of today's notes and write down everything that is important to you. Be honest and list the things you'd struggle to offer to God. Then pray and ask for God's help to offer these things to Him at the appropriate time.

CORE THEME | DISCIPLESHIP 1

Learner

READ: LUKE 10:38–42

KEY VERSE V39
'Mary… sat at the Lord's feet listening to what he said.'

The word for today is **Learner**. A disciple is someone who learns from their rabbi (a Jewish word that Jesus and the disciples would have used) or teacher. To be specific, in order to be a disciple of Christ we need to learn about Him and from Him. Knowing Jesus enables us to know the way to God. To know Jesus, we have to learn to have faith in His teaching, in the Bible and in the experience of the Holy Spirit.

Jesus said, 'If you knew me, you would know my Father also' (John 8:19). Jesus wants us to know more about Him. He isn't secretive or elusive – Jesus is eager for us to learn more about Him and is overjoyed when we do so. That's why He left the Holy Spirit to help us understand and remember what Jesus taught in the Bible. We may not be able to physically sit at Jesus' feet as Mary did, but we can adopt an attitude of learning and soak up His teaching from the Bible. By reading *Mettle* every day, you are showing the characteristics of a disciple – wanting to learn more about your faith. Keep going!

Discipleship Tip: Learn all you can about Jesus. It's OK to ask questions!

Pray

Holy Spirit, help me to grow in my faith. Teach me more about Jesus. I want to learn more about Him and the amazing love He has for me. Amen.

Weekend

5/6 SEP

Apprentice

READ: HEBREWS 11:1–13

KEY VERSE V1
'faith is confidence in what we hope for and assurance about what we do not see.'

The word today is **Apprentice**. Top athletes have coaches for every aspect of their game – even though they are already great at their sport, they will spend hours training; learning from their coaches and perfecting their skills. A star athlete constantly learns and strives to perform better. Jamie Oliver started his career as a catering apprentice and now he has a chain of restaurants, numerous books and apprentices learning from him. If you are willing to learn and have a great mentor, who knows what could happen in your future?

Yesterday we looked at the importance of learning and growing in our faith. But what is faith? It is the 'confidence in what we hope for and assurance about what we do not see' (Heb. 11:1, NLT). Today's verses go on to give examples of biblical characters who show great faith. Noah builds an enormous boat on land to save the animals and his family. Abraham leaves home to follow God's instructions, although he doesn't know where he will end up. These Old Testament characters were held up to the Early Church as having faith in God in difficult circumstances – and they are still great examples for us today.

Are you willing to be taught by others? The Christian apprentices in Hebrews didn't need to see the short-term end, they were focusing on the long term – an eternity spent with God.

Discipleship Tip: Be willing to be taught by others. Think about the idea of being mentored. Do you know someone older/wiser/more experienced than you, who you respect and could mentor you?

Pray

Father, thank You for the faithful example set by others. Help me to be an example to others, and grow in the confidence that You have good plans for me, even if I can't see how those plans will come about right now. Amen.

Scholar

READ: LUKE 10:25–37

KEY VERSE V26
'How do you read it?'

The word for today is **Scholar**. Today's reading is the well-known parable of the Good Samaritan. A man is beaten and left for dead. A priest and a Levite fail to help him but a Samaritan – a foreigner and traditionally an enemy of the Jews – stops to help. But go back to the start and notice why Jesus tells this story: because 'an expert in the law' (v25) asks a question. This man knows the Scriptures really well but he is still struggling to grasp the basics about loving God and loving others. Jesus initially replies by asking him a question: 'What do *you* think?'

Jesus loves it when we study the Bible and really try to understand it. It doesn't matter if we don't understand everything (and some of it is pretty strange!) but at least we are using our brains and having a go. The Bible has been studied for centuries and is still being studied. So let's study the Bible, ask questions, dig deep and be scholars.

Discipleship Tip: Study the Bible, get to know God's teaching and become a scholar who knows God deeply – not just enough to get by.

✚ *Challenge*

Have you got questions about the Bible and the Christian faith? Why not set up a small Bible study group and discuss them with others. Ask the Holy Spirit to be present too and nudge you towards the answers.

Supporter

READ: JOHN 17:3–4

KEY VERSE V3
'this is eternal life: that they know you, the only true God, and Jesus Christ, whom you have sent.'

The word for today is **Supporter**. How do we get the eternal life mentioned in today's reading? By knowing Jesus and understanding that it was God who sent Him to earth.

In the film *Finding Nemo**, Crush the turtle is having a conversation with Marlin the clownfish about trusting and letting go. Marlin asks him: 'But when do you know?' and the response is: 'You know when you know, you know?' At which point they both nod knowingly, but then a confused look crosses Marlin's face.

When do we know 'the only true God, and Jesus'? It's the same answer: 'You know when you know, you know?' You can have all the facts laid out, but when you're filled with the Holy Spirit, you experience a new dimension of knowing God. Being a supporter means getting to know who you support better and better, which engages your emotions as well as your mind.

Discipleship Tip: Being a supporter also usually means that you tell people about who you support and why. Tell others about God, and understand that it is His Holy Spirit who reveals who He is to them.

Pray

Father, I want to know You more and to know Your presence in my life. Help me to recognise You and to tell others about You every day. Amen.

*Finding Nemo, Walt Disney/Pixar, 2003

CORE THEME | DISCIPLESHIP 1

Piecing the clues together

READ: JOHN 17:6–8

KEY VERSE V7
'Now they know that everything you have given me comes from you.'

What does it mean to be a disciple? For Jesus' disciples, it meant having some incredible experiences, but it also meant being challenged on what they believed.

Jesus and His disciples spent three years together: travelling, teaching and testifying. The disciples saw Jesus do amazing things: from feeding the 5,000 to sharing water with the woman at the well; from walking on water to calming a storm; from healing the Roman officer's servant to bringing Lazarus back to life.

However, it was only in the last few months together that Jesus actually challenged them to say who they believed Him to be (Matt. 16:15–16). And only in the last few days did Jesus draw together all of what the disciples had seen and heard. As we follow Jesus, it's helpful to look back on what He's done for us and what it means. In doing so we get fresh insights into who Jesus really is.

Discipleship Tip: Make time to think about what you have learnt about God. Try keeping a journal to jot down anything you find really interesting or helpful.

Think

Like in a detective movie, sometimes the clues don't make sense until the last minute. Jesus was confirming to God that His disciples knew Him; knew He had come from God and now knew that everything He had done was through God.

CORE THEME | DISCIPLESHIP 1

13

He knows

≡ **READ: JOHN 17:9–10**

KEY VERSE V9
'I am not praying for the world, but for those you have given me'

In today's reading, Jesus is praying for those who know Him. Not for everybody in the whole world, but specifically for those He has spent time with, and especially the ones who know Him personally – the disciples who were with Him then and His disciples now... that's you!

Jesus has time for everybody – but here He prays for those He knows. He knows His disciples really well and what they struggle with: James' and John's hot tempers, Peter's impulsiveness and rashness, Thomas and his questions. And He knows how to deal with them. To Peter, Jesus says: 'Before the cock crows today, you will deny three times that you know me' (Luke 22:34), and to Thomas He says, 'Reach out your hand and put it into my side' (John 20:27).

Jesus knows about you and cares about you as well. He knows what doubts you have and what you find hard to get your head round – and He knows how to deal with your struggles too. That's a really important part of being a disciple.

Discipleship Tip: Jesus knows you personally as an individual and really does care a lot about you. It's good to remember that.

🕮 *Think*

If you know Jesus, He knows you as well and is praying for you. He knows exactly what you are going through and is praying to the Father that you handle it. Ask for help and be confident that He is praying for you.

Passing it on

READ: JOHN 17:21–26

KEY VERSE V26
*'I have made you known to them, and will continue
to make you known'*

If God has been revealed to you by Jesus, what are you
going to do about it? Today's chapter ends with a promise
from Jesus: He will continue to reveal Himself. We know
that this prayer is not just for the disciples way back then,
but for us as disciples now. No one knows everything
there is to know about God, but He is more than happy for
us to get to know Him and Jesus has promised to keep on
revealing more and more of God to us.

As disciples, we have been given the challenge to pass
on the knowledge to our friends, family and those around
us. It sounds really hard, but with Jesus on our side, is it
really that difficult?

Let's look back at what we've learned about discipleship
so far in this section of *Mettle*. Think about all you've read.
Go over the Discipleship Tips and remind yourself of what
we've discovered: He created us for a reason, He wants
us to learn about Him, He knows us individually, He cares
about us and He is praying for us. How do these things
make you feel about following Jesus and telling other
people about Him?

Discipleship Tip: As a disciple, desire every day to learn
more about Jesus; then put what you discover into practice.

Pray
*Father, reveal more of Yourself to me today, so that I may be
able to talk to others about You, the God who lives in me. Amen.*

CORE THEME | DISCIPLESHIP 1

**WEEKEND
12/13 SEP**

PEER PRESSURE

The pressure's on!
READ: GENESIS 3:1–7

KEY VERSE V6
'she took some and ate it. She also gave some to her husband, who was with her, and he ate it.'

Over the next couple of weeks, we're going to be looking at the hot topic of peer pressure. What is it? How does it happen? What effect does it have on us? Then, later on, in Part Two, we take a look at how we can face and deal with peer pressure head-on.

So, when did it all start? Well, the first instance of peer pressure comes pretty quickly after creation. Eve takes a bite from the forbidden fruit, and then passes it on to Adam – now what should he do? Should he tell her he doesn't like that type of fruit and risk what happens next, or should he take a bite, even though he knows full well he shouldn't? So many factors to take into account, so many reasons to go one way or the other – all over a very simple question: does he eat the fruit or not?

Each of us will face tricky decisions on a regular basis. They probably won't have anything to do with fruit, but they will involve us having to make a choice! What will motivate our decisions? Are we going to decide what to do based on what people around us do, say and think? Or are we going to base our choices on something else, something deeper? No one is saying that this is an easy question, but it's an important one to get to grips with.

Think

As we start looking at the issue of peer pressure, spend a few moments in quiet, with God. Think about the situations that force you to make the choice between leading and being led by others. Think about how God might be able to show you another path.

In denial

≡ **READ: MATTHEW 26:69–75**

KEY VERSE V70
'But he denied it before them all. "I don't know what you're talking about," he said.'

It's easy to feel a bit sorry for Peter. He was a decent guy who had done his best to follow Jesus. However, in today's reading he makes a major mistake, and it's laid bare for all to read . We know he makes up for it later on, but still – we probably wouldn't like our own failures recorded so publicly.

Peter was faced with a problem: he knew he should remain faithful to Jesus, just as he promised he would, but he was also terrified of what might happen if he was seen to be 'one of them' – one of Jesus' disciples. Sadly, he found the pressure just too much… and he gave in. Today we read of how Peter gets quite angry as he lies to the people around him, maintaining that he is not a follower of Jesus.

Faced with the pressure to identify with a group on the 'outside', we might hope we would stand up under that pressure, but would we? What would it take to make us fold; to give up and pretend to be someone we're not? How often in school or out with our mates are we scared about what might happen if we tell the truth? Peter's declaration reminds us that it takes real courage in the face of extreme peer pressure to stand up for what we believe in. Could we withstand the pressure?

HOT TOPIC | PEER PRESSURE 1

➕ ## *Challenge*

Spend a few moments asking God to forgive you for the times when peer pressure has made you scared and you've not been faithful to what you believe.

Culture shock!

READ: DANIEL 1:1–16

KEY VERSE V8
'Daniel… asked the head of the palace staff to exempt him from the royal diet.' (The Message)

Every community has certain customs and rituals of its own. Whether it's our class at school, our football team or our drama group, the group will do things because that's the way they've 'always done them'. These customs or traditions are passed on from old to new members, and are often taken for granted. But sometimes there comes a moment when we have to stop and think: is what they've always done right – and is it right for me?

Daniel and his friends, prisoners in a foreign land, found themselves having to learn a new language and a new culture. Part of the culture involved consuming the same food and drink as the others working at the palace. However, Daniel and his friends wanted to obey God's laws about clean and unclean food, which meant limiting themselves to fruit and veg (their five-a-day) rather than eating what was being offered.

Despite the pressure to conform, Daniel battled against custom and proved that God's way was better. How often do we just do what we've always done rather than doing something new, something better? Tradition can be a good thing, but it's sometimes just the pressure to keep things as they've always been.

 ## Pray
Dear God, help me to do what is right and to follow Your way. Give me strength to continue to live for You. Amen.

HOT TOPIC | PEER PRESSURE 1

Crowd control

READ: MARK 15:6–15

KEY VERSE V11
'But the chief priests stirred up the crowd to get Pilate to release Barabbas instead.'

'Why did you do that?' asks the teacher. 'Everyone else was doing it, sir,' replies the student. How many times has a conversation similar to this taken place in schools up and down the country? Group mentality can be a dangerous thing – people in a crowd do and say things they would never dream of doing on their own.

Today's passage is a chilling reminder of what can happen when peer pressure takes over a crowd. As individuals, if asked, many of those there in front of Pontius Pilate might have given the 'Get out of jail free' card to Jesus rather than to a convicted criminal and murderer. As it was, a little pressure from the local religious leaders and, all of a sudden, the crowd were baying for Jesus' blood. We don't know whether the chief priests threatened, bribed or reasoned with those present, but the pressure they exerted was obvious.

Are you someone who goes along with the crowd? Do you get caught up in the group mentality and find that you're doing or saying things because everyone else is? Being the one who says no in a crowd of people saying yes can be really hard, but there's comfort in knowing that you've had the courage to think for yourself.

 Pray

Lord, please give me the boldness to do what You would have me do. Watch over me when I find I need to go against what everyone else is doing. Amen.

HOT TOPIC | PEER PRESSURE 1

Best laid plans

 READ: EXODUS 32:1–6

KEY VERSE V1
'When the people saw that Moses was so long in coming down from the mountain, they gathered round Aaron'

The Israelites were tired, hungry, thirsty and fed up. They'd left Egypt ready for something new, something better. What they'd got was desert, desert and more desert. Now Moses, their leader, had left them and wandered off up a mountain. All in all, they were getting a bit irritated with the whole thing.

Moses' brother, Aaron, was left to deal with an increasingly disaffected people, who wanted immediate guidance. They didn't know when Moses was due back, so they decided to try to get the direction they wanted from idols made of gold. Aaron must have known this wasn't the best of plans, but he also knew that objecting to their idea wouldn't go down well. So he agreed, and the Israelites ended up in a whole new heap of trouble.

You might ask why Aaron didn't just tell the Israelites to be patient and wait until Moses returned. Peer pressure can sometimes feel very threatening. We don't want to let down the people around us, nor to find out what will happen if we do, so we end up doing things we'd never have dreamed of. However, we need to remember the bigger picture and ask God to give us the strength we need to follow Him.

 Think

How would things be different if the next time you felt peer pressure or wanted to pressure someone else, you stopped and asked yourself what God would want to come from the situation?

HOT TOPIC | PEER PRESSURE 1

Just because

≡ **READ: DANIEL 3:1–30**

KEY VERSE V7
'as they heard the sound… all the nations and peoples of every language fell down and worshipped the image of gold'

→ A long time ago now, there was an advert aiming to discourage young people from smoking. It showed some teenagers doing all the things teen smokers do but, rather than having cigarettes, they had party noisemakers.

The sight of these teenagers rushing into the toilets to have a quick blow on kazoo-like toys came across as pretty odd, highlighting the fact that smoking is, in reality, a really strange thing to do! Now, many of you may be sitting there proudly saying to yourselves: 'Aha! I don't smoke. It doesn't interest me.' But how often do we do something just as inexplicable – just because the people around us are doing it?

There's something about the effects of peer pressure that seems to rob otherwise intelligent people of their common sense. People will wear completely off-the-wall combinations of clothes, just because everyone's wearing them. They'll buy particular things, or listen to particular music, just because it's the fashion – regardless of the logic behind their choices. Sometimes we need to stop and think about the things we do just to fit in. What do you do just because…?

HOT TOPIC | PEER PRESSURE 1

Think

Spend some time reflecting on how peer pressure leads you to do things you'd never contemplate normally. Ask God to help you be bold enough to take a different path.

Weekend

19/20 SEP

Want, want, want

READ: 1 JOHN 2:15–17

≡ KEY VERSE V16
'For everything in the world – the lust of the flesh, the lust of the eyes, and the pride of life – comes not from the Father but from the world.'

➝ While watching TV, you'll notice that advert after advert shows you loads of stuff you might want. Another games console, an amazing phone, the latest clothing lines, an exciting new movie – the list of desirable objects goes on and on and on. There is a tremendous pressure to own the latest phone or possess this season's most popular trainers.

This pressure is increased when it's not just the media prodding us to own these things but also the people around us. We see what others have – and we want it. Our friend is the first in the class to own the latest smart phone, and it seems pretty awesome – so we want it too. Everyone else seems to have a particular make of shoes – so we just have to have them as well! If we're honest, we can be pretty unimaginative when it comes to the stuff we think we want.

Today's Bible verses sum it up quite nicely – the world offers us a craving for physical pleasure and for the things we see around us. However, we are called to crave something very different. God wants us to seek the things of His kingdom rather than unnecessary material things.

We are called to withstand the constant pressure from the media and from our peers to buy, buy, buy and are asked to think about what it is we give, give, give. How do we contribute to the world around us? How do we make our schools and communities a little bit more how Jesus would want them?

Challenge

Is there something you're considering buying that you don't really need? How about using some of the money or your time to give something back to your community?

Practice makes perfect

 READ: PSALM 52:1–9

KEY VERSE V1
'Why do you boast of evil, you mighty hero?'

How many of us would consider ourselves expert liars? They say practice makes perfect and, if we're brave enough to admit it, some of us will have had a lot of practice at lying to those around us. Most of them are probably small lies – ones we don't really notice, but let's look at why they can be a problem.

The trouble is, it can often be much easier to lie than to tell the truth. There can often be huge pressure on us to say we've done certain things, or that we watch certain things online, and the easiest way to save face in these situations is just to lie about it. 'Did you see that video so-and-so posted last night?' 'Ah, yeah, it was great.'

We know that everyone else watched it and, even though we might not have wanted to watch it, it's easier to lie to our friends to save face, rather than admit the truth about what we like and dislike. The trouble is: little lies lead to bigger lies, and more dangerous lies, and before long we're caught up in a situation where we've told so many lies we can't remember which ones we've told. Just think how liberating it might feel to just tell the truth.

 ## Challenge
Make a conscious effort today to speak the truth and resist those 'white lies'.

Body talk

≡ **READ: 1 CORINTHIANS 6:12–20**

KEY VERSE V18
'Flee from sexual immorality. All other sins a person commits are outside the body, but whoever sins sexually, sins against their own body.'

It's used to sell chocolate, to add cheap laughs to sitcoms, sell make-up and to convince us that we really need the latest perfume or deodorant – whether we like it or not, we're surrounded by references to sex. And with that comes a huge pressure to be having it!

The later you get in your teen years, the more people seem to be sleeping with their boyfriend or girlfried, and the odder you might feel if you're not. For many, having sex isn't a big deal – it's something teenagers do, and you may feel weird or get teased by others if you're not. God created sex for human beings to enjoy – so if you've always believed that God's a prude, He really isn't! But, what sets us apart as followers of Jesus is how we 'steward' the gift of sex. Remember that whenever God puts boundaries around anything, it's for our benefit, not so spoil our fun! And, based on what the big picture of the Bible seems to suggest, sex is a gift best unwrapped within the safety and security of marriage, where two people can give themselves to each other for the rest of their lives.

Think about the boundaries you want to put in place to make sure you can keep sex as a holy and good thing for the long-haul. Why not spend some time praying about it? God won't be embarassed!

Pray
God, thank You that You created us to be sexual beings. Help me to trust that You know what's best for me. Amen.

HOT TOPIC | PEER PRESSURE 1

Walk this way

 READ: 2 TIMOTHY 4:1–8

KEY VERSE V2
'preach the word; be prepared in season and out of season; correct, rebuke and encourage – with great patience and careful instruction'

→ Today's verse in full is quite a mouthful! There's an awful lot contained in a fairly short sentence, but it leaves us with a huge challenge. It introduces the idea that peer pressure might not always be a bad thing.

There might be times when it's your job to use your influence on the people around you. In the same way that we know we don't always get it right ourselves, there are times when those around us would really benefit from a careful prod in the right direction.

Today's verse tells us that we are called to correct, rebuke and encourage. We are told that we should point out what's not right, show others how it can be made right, and encourage them to get it right. And all this should be done with 'great patience and careful instruction' (v2).

You might know what it's like to teach someone to do something, and maybe you'll have felt frustration when people don't get it right first time. It's not hard to prod them back in the right direction (or tell them where they went wrong); the hard bit is to do it in love, with patience.

 Think

If a friend you trusted and respected was to 'correct', 'rebuke' or 'encourage' you, how would you like them to do so? What kind of language would get through to you? Try to hold that in mind should you ever feel led to talk to someone else about their decisions or behaviour. And don't forget to pray about it first!

HOT TOPIC | PEER PRESSURE 1

Bed head

 READ: HEBREWS 10:19–25

KEY VERSE V24
'And let us consider how we may spur one another on towards love and good deeds'

What keeps you going? For a lot of us, just getting out of bed in the morning can be a real struggle – the bed is so warm and comfortable! However, on the days when we know we have something special to look forward to, we're out of bed like a shot!

Peer pressure can have you in the first category – wanting to stay in bed and not face the day. It can feel relentless, and withstanding its influence can leave you unpopular – and sometimes unhappy! What you need is some motivation.

Today's verse encourages its readers to be original in finding ways of motivating others to do what God wants. Each of us needs encouragement to give us the strength to carry on. If we encourage other people, they will encourage us, and we'll find that the journey is just a little bit easier. It might not make it any easier to get out of bed in the morning, but it might make the task of standing up against peer pressure a little more bearable.

 ## *Challenge*

How can you use your influence to motivate others to 'love and good works'? Who are you going to encourage this week? Resolve to use your influence to encourage someone to carry out a kind and selfless act this week.

HOT TOPIC | PEER PRESSURE 1

Decisions, decisions!

 **READ: MATTHEW 6:19–34**

KEY VERSE V24
'No one can serve two masters. Either you will hate the one and love the other, or you will be devoted to the one and despise the other.'

→ So, it boils down to this: the final page of Part One of our topic 'Peer Pressure'. No one can serve two masters. Peer pressure is all about choices – big choices, little choices, easy choices, complicated choices – all kinds of choices. Peer pressure tries to take away our ability to make our own decisions, by pressurising us to decide based on what others think or do.

Today's key verse makes it clear that this isn't a good way to live. We can either be people who make our decisions based on our faith, or we can be people who make our decisions based on the actions and influences of others. On paper, this might seem to be an obvious choice – the right answer just jumps off the page. However, in practice we know that it isn't always that easy.

There'll be some days when we make the right choice – our decisions are based on what we know God would want. On other days, we'll be desperate to do what our friends do and will let our choices be influenced by our peers. Let's aim to have more days when God is directing our path than days when it's the people around us who are directing us.

↑ Pray
Dear God, help me to make my choices based on what You would want, rather than on what the people around me would choose. Amen.

HOT TOPIC | PEER PRESSURE 1

HUMOUR

Live happy!

READ: JOHN 10:1–10

KEY VERSE V10
'I have come that they may have life, and have it to the full.'

Humour is a weird and wonderful thing. The most random things can set us off, and half the time the 'funny' can't even be explained. What one person laughs at just leaves another confused. But good humour and pure laughter make life richer and more enjoyable. They are part of God's character and as we are His creations, they are part of ours too.

That might come as a surprise to some people who think that being a Christian means living a boring life bound by a bunch of do's and don'ts. But Christians are supposed to be the freest and happiest people on earth! Because the more you know how incredibly loved by God you are – and the more you discover what an amazing life He has planned for you – the more confident, joyful and hope-filled you become.

Some other Bible versions translate John 10:10, which talks about God's desire to give us a 'full life', as 'everything in abundance, more than you expect — life in its fullness until you overflow!' (TPT) and 'real and eternal life, more and better life than they ever dreamed of' (*The Message*).

God warns us there will be difficulties in this life, but He also promises that anyone who believes in Jesus – in who He is and what He has done for us – and leans into God for strength and guidance, will find that they have all that they need in life and more. That includes humour and joy! Whether it's sharing a moment, a smile or even an eye-watering, shoulder-shaking laugh, which can set you off again days later just at the memory of it.

Think

It feels so good to smile, to laugh. What are some of your funniest memories? Who did you get to share that moment with? Check your face... you're probably smiling now, just at the memory of laughing!

Get the giggles

READ: ECCLESIASTES 3:9–14

KEY VERSE V12
'there is nothing better for people than to be happy and to do good while they live.'

HOT TOPIC | HUMOUR 1

Have you ever noticed that laughter is contagious? Sometimes just watching someone else having a fit of the giggles is enough to get you going too, even if you have no idea what the original joke was! What about when you're mad at someone and you really want to stay mad, but they are doing something goofy to make you smile and you end up letting go of your anger and laughing in spite of yourself... They're good moments, aren't they? Who really wants to stay angry anyway?

Good humour is a gift from God – He *wants* us to be able to find moments of happiness in each and every day, no matter what else is going on. When we are busy and under pressure from school, peers or family expectations, we often forget to take time to let go, enjoy life and have a really good laugh. Laughter is created by God to remind us of the joy He has in us. It's essential to our wellbeing for a reason! So even in the middle of your hard work and daily chores, rip open this gift He's given you and think of all the reasons He's given you to smile.

Challenge

Like laughter, smiling can be contagious too. Try wearing a smile as you walk along the street, or through the halls at school. Sometimes all it takes is a smile – from a friend or a stranger – to brighten up someone's day.

Time to party!

READ: ACTS 2:42–47

KEY VERSE V42

'They devoted themselves to the apostles' teaching and to fellowship, to the breaking of bread and to prayer.'

Let's break that verse down a bit. Basically the believers got together to hear the good (amazing!) news about Jesus, to hang out, to eat and to pray. Verse 47 adds that they were glad – as in *really* happy – and that every day more and more people joined the party. That's some kind of draw they had!

Why? Because the believers had something that everyone wanted to be a part of. Their relationships were so strong that everyone felt loved and included. Their generosity meant that no one was in need. Their prayers weren't timid and small – they were filled with God's power so that people were getting healed of sickness, released from depression and demons were getting cast out exactly as Jesus had instructed His disciples to do (Matt. 10:8). Who wouldn't want to be part of a group bursting with so much joy and so many incredible stories?

If you've ever had a few days away with your friends, your church or youth group, you'll know that something funny will often happen during those few days and people will be telling the story about it for years to come. 'Do you remember when…?' That's how it was with the Early Church – we are still telling some of their stories today!

HOT TOPIC | HUMOUR 1

Pray

Lord Jesus, thank You that You really know how to have fun. Help me to become more aware of Your presence in day-to-day life, and to learn how to have a really good laugh with You. Amen.

Let it all out

≡ **READ: ECCLESIASTES 3:1–8**

KEY VERSE V4
'a time to weep and a time to laugh'

Life is full of ups and downs and sometimes we want to turn our backs on God when things are tough, because we don't understand why He allows us to suffer.

In this passage however, we read that feeling low is a part of life for everyone. (Sorry, that's not quite what you wanted to hear, hey?) In fact the book of Psalm, like Ecclesiastes here, are full of the breadth and depth of emotion – from pain to joy, from anger with God to rejoicing and praising Him. This is what it means to be fully human.

It's true that God gives us the gifts of joy and humour even in the midst of our struggles, but He also understands our pain, sorrow and confusion. He is so compassionate that He came to live on earth – of course to save us by His grace and sacrifice, but also so that we could know that He had been through every human emotion Himself (Heb. 2:17; 4:15). He understands how we feel and He wants us to bring even our darkest thoughts and emotions to Him so that He can comfort us and guide us through. He can even handle it when we rant and rave at Him – He will never turn His back on us.

➕ ## Challenge

Are you experiencing a 'time to cry' at the moment? It's OK to not be OK. Talk to God about it. Look for a wise and trustworthy person He's put in your world – simply sharing a struggle can help lighten the load.

HOT TOPIC | HUMOUR 1

Happy chemicals

READ: PROVERBS 17:17–28

KEY VERSE V22
'A cheerful heart is good medicine, but a crushed spirit dries up the bones.'

Proverbs is known as 'the book of wisdom' – practical tips on how to live life to the full, God's way. Our language may have changed over time, but the wisdom remains the same. Verse 22 offers some fun advice – that laughter is actually healing!

Scientists are discovering the truth of this ancient yet absolutely present reality, so much so that 'Laughter Therapy' is a recognised and recommended method of treatment for overcoming stress and stress-induced disorders. Laughter decreases the level of stress hormones that build up in our bodies and increases the levels of endorphins or 'happy chemicals' (the natural, healthy type!) which are released when we laugh.

Although laughing is sometimes the last thing you feel like doing, the idea that it might actually help offers much needed light and hope! Life isn't about what happens to us – it's about how we respond to the things that happen. There are countless stories of inspirational people who have been through immense horror and hardship, yet a positive outlook and thankful heart despite the circumstances has kept them going.

Think

Positive thinking is biblical, and so is laughter. Instead of dwelling on the negative, focus your thoughts on what's good in your situation, and thank God for it!

HOT TOPIC | HUMOUR 1

Bring it!

READ: LUKE 6:17–36

KEY VERSE V21
'Blessed are you who weep now, for you will laugh.'

Heaven – the real heaven, not the Victorian painting version filled with chubby cherubs – sounds awesome. It's a place with no pain, no depression, no sickness, no sorrow, no death. There's no poverty or need because even the roads are paved with gold and the walls are laid with gemstones reflecting light of every colour in every direction. A place of music and laughter where the partying never ends (Rev. 21).

Exciting as this may be for our future, as followers of Jesus we have been tasked with an imperative mission while here on earth – to bring about God's kingdom in the here and now. See, the kingdom of heaven is not some remote place in a distant future: it's *inside* us. God has built into us creativity, kindness, grace, forgiveness, ability, brilliance, strength, character, humour and so much more. Every time we think, speak or act in a way which reflects how God created us to be and helps someone in our world, we are bringing a bit more of heaven to earth.

Inspired by the knowledge that we are both loved and empowered by God, we can bring comfort to the crying. We can help with encouraging words, open arms, practical help, creative solutions and even humour.

Pray

Is there anyone you know who might need some encouragement today? Pray for an opportunity for God to bring laughter and love to them through you.

HOT TOPIC | HUMOUR 1

Weekend

3/4 OCT

What on earth?

READ: GENESIS 1:1–25

KEY VERSE V25

'God made the wild animals according to their kinds, the livestock according to their kinds, and all the creatures that move along the ground according to their kinds. And God saw that it was good.'

When God created our world, He declared it to be 'good'. Not good as in 'adequate' or 'achieves expectations', but good as in *completely* good, absent of any defect and mind-blowingly wonderful! We'd translate it to something more like 'awesome'... which it was! And in all that awesome goodness, there is diversity beyond belief! God created all of it for us to discover, wonder at, laugh at, nurture and protect. Have you ever watched nature programmes or explored nature for yourself and marvelled over how bizarre and awkward some of the creatures on our fabulous planet are? There's the blue-bottomed baboon, the duck-billed platypus, the aye-aye rodent and numerous other strange and wonderful creatures…

Let's not miss the fun of God's creation by taking it for granted, neglecting it or ruining it. God was intentional about creating it – now it's our privilege and our responsibility to be intentional about exploring, appreciating and protecting this stunning planet God has entrusted us with.

When was the last time you stopped to appreciate the natural world right outside your front door? Take some time this weekend to look for and notice the beauty around you and imagine God laughing with delight as He crafted it all – for you. Thank Him for some part of it, whether it's a field crisp and covered in morning frost, a flower defiantly growing up between grey paving slabs, waves lapping on sand or crashing on rocks… whatever it is that makes you just go, 'Wow!'

Pray

Walk through your neighbourhood. Go slow. Literally breathe in God's goodness. Ask God to open your eyes, your heart and your mind to the wonder of His creation, and to teach you about life as you revel in the beauty and detail of all He has made. Thank Him… and share in His joy.

Taking prisoners!

 READ: 2 CORINTHIANS 10:2–11

KEY VERSE V5
'we take captive every thought to make it obedient to Christ.'

What's the most repeated command in the Bible? 'Do not worry. Don't be afraid. Rejoice! Give thanks! Praise the Lord!' Wait – that's more than one! Why? Because they all stem from the same root – trust in the Lord, and in doing so, *be happy!*

God knows that His children flourish most in life when we live from a mindset of joy. That's why it's a common theme all through the Scriptures. Jesus – our example for victorious living – was able to endure the greatest agony ever known because of the joy set before Him (Heb.12:2). And what was that joy? It was *you,* brought into right relationship with God through Jesus, and reigning in life because of it. Wow.

So how do we follow Christ's example? By taking everything life throws at us – circumstances, labels, even thoughts – and bringing it to Jesus, to see what He says about it. Say you've been labelled (by yourself or others) as stupid: what does the Word say? He says you have the mind of Christ – the greatest mind ever (1 Cor. 2:16)! And when life is tough, does that mean it's all bad? Nope! God wants to help you through it, to grow and become even more amazing through adversity (James 1:2–5).

HOT TOPIC | HUMOUR 1

 ## *Challenge*

Write down a thought you're struggling with. Search for that word on biblegateway.com to find out what God says about it. Write down God's truth and reread it daily until the joy of it sinks in.

The ridiculous to the sublime

READ: GENESIS 18:12–25

KEY VERSE V12
'So Sarah laughed to herself as she thought, "After I am worn out and my lord is old, will I now have this pleasure?"'

→ Sarah scoffed at God (which was either very brave or very foolish). But honestly, if you were in your nineties and someone said you were going to have a baby, you'd laugh in their face too. The idea seemed so ridiculous, how could she have any other response?

But God responded, 'Is anything too hard for the Lord?' (v14). Sure enough, one year later, along comes the original bundle of joy – appropriately named Isaac, meaning 'laughter'. Sarah learned through experience that God's plans are never impossible, however laughable they seem, and that He is always true to His word. Certainly, she knew that God had made her sublimely happy (Gen. 21:6–7).

Some things never change: just as He did over and over in biblical times, God still loves to make seemingly ridiculous, impossible plans and promises for our lives today. Plans beyond our wildest dreams. The other thing that hasn't changed: He is still *always* faithful to bring them about. So, *is* anything too hard for the Lord?

Think

Is there an area in your life where you are doubting God? Reread today's scripture and replace your doubts with a declaration of God's faithfulness and ability to bring about the dreams that He has put in your heart.

HOT TOPIC | HUMOUR 1

Keys to the kingdom

 READ: MATTHEW 19:13–30

KEY VERSE V14

'Jesus said, "Let the little children come to me, and do not hinder them, for the kingdom of heaven belongs to such as these."'

While Sarah laughed at the seemingly impossible, there's a group of humanity for whom nothing ever seems impossible. A group of people who instinctively embrace all things fun and silly; who know how to 'dream big' without ever considering logistics or laws of nature or the opinions of others; who trust easily and laugh the most. Little children.

When others dismissed them and tried to shoo these 'unimportant' individuals away, Jesus defended them, welcomed them with open arms, and warned all the grown-ups present that they had better learn once again how to be like little children – for the heartbeat of heaven lives in their character traits. Young children not only laugh a lot but they also forgive quickly, trust unwaveringly, love to learn (that constant question 'Why...?'), find fun in simplicity and don't care what others think about them. Maybe that's why they are so happy. And if we think about it, isn't this what Jesus wants us to do? To rejoice always, forgive as we've been forgiven, trust in the Lord, be taught by the Holy Spirit, store up treasure in heaven and find our identity in Christ?

 Challenge

Next time you're around a small child, watch, listen and learn. We all tend to develop inhibitions and defences as we 'grow up', but how can you 'grow down' a little instead?

HOT TOPIC | HUMOUR 1

From the ~~horse's~~ donkey's mouth

READ: NUMBERS 22:21–41

KEY VERSE V28

'Then the LORD opened the donkey's mouth, and it said to Balaam, "What have I done to you to make you beat me these three times?"'

A talking donkey? God does communicate with us in funny ways sometimes! (Also weird: Balaam seems completely unsurprised that his donkey can speak!) God had to go to extremes to get through to Balaam, as Balaam was so determined to ignore Him.

God had already told Balaam not to go and curse the Israelites (v12), but Balaam responded with compromise rather than total obedience (v18). He refused to go with the officials, yet told them to stay the night, hoping God might change His mind (v19). Seeing that Balaam still longed to persist in making wealth through the occult, God said, 'Fine, have it your way. Go, and see what happens' (v20 paraphrase). Thinking that he's twisted God's arm, Balaam jumps up the next morning and goes arrogantly on his way (v21), until he is stopped in his tracks, literally – by a donkey.

You know you're in trouble when God has to use an ass to get through to you. Hopefully God doesn't have to go to such extremes to get us! So how does He communicate with us? Often He 'speaks' through the Bible as we soak up His Word and His presence. This takes intentionality on our part to make time and space to hang out with Him and listen to Him.

Pray

Make time to pray today. Give God space to speak and listen to what He has to say – then be ready to respond.

HOT TOPIC | HUMOUR 1

Toilet humour

≡ **READ: 1 KINGS 18:16–40**

KEY VERSE V27
'About noontime Elijah began mocking them. "You'll have to shout louder," he scoffed, "for surely he is a god! Perhaps he is daydreaming, or is relieving himself."' (NLT)

Toilet humour is not a new thing. Many years BC, Elijah suggests that maybe Baal, the god worshipped by the people of Israel, is not answering their prayers because he is taking a leak. Elijah is courageous enough and confident enough in God that he ridicules the prophets of Baal. He even goes as far as pouring water over the unlit wood before asking God to set fire to it. Is he mad, or full of himself? Or is he actually just incredibly full of faith?

The Israelites who were watching while Elijah doused the Lord's altar with water must certainly have thought he was out of his mind. They would definitely have been laughing and shaking their heads at him. It took the absurdity of the situation to wipe the smirks off their faces as they realised they'd been following an impotent false deity instead of the all-powerful, one true God.

But before we laugh too hard at the Israelites, we need to ask ourselves: Am I putting *all* my trust and faith in almighty God for the details of my life, or am I trying to find security and reassurance in someone or something else? It's so easy for us to fall into the trap of trusting in our own abilities or strength – they can become our idol, our Baal, without us even realising.

HOT TOPIC | HUMOUR 1

🝳 *Think*

Are you putting your trust in human effort or creations, or are you trusting heart and soul in God alone?

01

**WEEKEND
10/11 OCT**

OBEDIENCE

The Jesus way

READ: JAMES 4:1–10

KEY VERSE V7
'Submit yourselves, then, to God.'

Obedience is not fashionable. In many ways, our culture urges us to do what we want; to insist on our rights, make ourselves comfortable and ignore anyone who tells us to do things their way. The idea of obeying someone else – not just listening to that person, but constantly obeying them – can seem strange to people around us. But this is Jesus' way. Following Jesus means doing what God wants, not just what we want. It means serving other people, not ourselves, and focusing more on our responsibilities rather than our rights.

Obeying someone can feel uncomfortable. Submitting to anyone can sound like a very negative concept. Choosing to submit to someone makes us feel vulnerable. So why is it a good thing for us to submit to God? In the next two weeks, we'll explore some answers to this question and think about exactly what obeying God means for us.

For now, these verses from James reassure us that God can be trusted with our obedience. As we come to God and let Him rule our lives, He will come close to us (v8), and if we choose to make ourselves humble, He will honour us. We can trust God to care for us and do what is best for us. So we needn't be afraid to submit to Him, obey Him and make ourselves vulnerable to Him. God loves us, wants to bless us and only wants to be in control of us because His plans are always better than our own.

Pray

Ask God to show you what obeying Him really means. Be patient, listen and see what He has to say. Choose to submit to Him, even if that takes you outside your comfort zone.

Take it easy?

READ: JOB 22:21–30

KEY VERSE V21
'Submit to God and be at peace with him; in this way prosperity will come to you.'

At first look, this verse seems to say that God is like a vending machine. If you put a coin in a vending machine, out comes a chocolate bar. If you submit to God, out comes peace, happiness and an easy life. So does this verse really mean that if we obey God, life will always be easy? Unfortunately not!

Living for God is about having a relationship with Him, not about what we can get out of Him. And God certainly doesn't guarantee us an easy life. Many of us know people who have chosen to submit to God completely and then faced some really hard times. We might even have experienced that ourselves. But our key verse does reassure us that God's way is always the best way.

Trusting in God won't necessarily make us rich, famous or popular but, even if life is hard, we will find true peace and real purpose if we obey Him wholeheartedly.

Challenge

Are you obeying God wholeheartedly? Or are you holding back in case He asks you to do something you don't really want to do? Choose today to submit to God, whatever happens. Remember, you can trust Him to know what's best for you!

HOT TOPIC | OBEDIENCE 1

Lightbulb moment!

 READ: LUKE 5:1–11

KEY VERSE V5
'we've worked hard all night and haven't caught anything. But because you say so, I will let down the nets.'

You might know that the first electric light bulb was invented by Thomas Edison. What you might *not* know is that Edison got through hundreds of unsuccessful designs before finally producing a working light bulb in October 1879. There must have been days when trying another slightly different design must have seemed to Edison like the last thing he should do. Trying something completely different or just giving up would have seemed far wiser. And yet, he persevered – and the result was something amazing. The disciples might have felt something similar. They had fished all night and caught nothing. To repeat almost exactly what they'd been doing already made no sense at all! But even though Peter knew very little about Jesus, he realised that Jesus had real authority, so he trusted Him. When Peter acts on his trust and does what Jesus says, the results are amazing.

Obeying Jesus means doing what He says, even when it doesn't immediately seem wise. Jesus can give us new insights for tough situations. Sometimes this might mean a surprising new option. At other times, it might just mean carrying on when we feel like giving up. Either way, if we obey Jesus, we can trust His way to be the wisest. The results can be spectacular!

HOT TOPIC | OBEDIENCE 1

 Think

What are you struggling with at the moment? What might Jesus be saying about how to solve the problem?

Off-limits?

READ: MATTHEW 22:34–40

KEY VERSE V40
'All the Law and the Prophets hang on these two commandments.'

A husband, if he is feeling romantic, might buy his wife a bunch of flowers. Some mornings, he might get up and make his wife a cup of tea, then take it to her in bed. At the weekend, he might take the kids out for a while, to give his wife some time to herself. And he might make sure that he always spends at least one evening a week with her and no one else.

This might sound like a relationship that is simply a list of stuff to do. Of course, there's far more to it than that. When we love someone, we don't do these sorts of things just for the sake of doing them, or because we think we ought to. We do them because we love the other person and want to make him or her happy. As we get to know our loved ones, we realise what things make them happy.

Living for God is similar to this. It's about far more than doing what look like good things and not doing what look like bad things: it's about getting to know and love Him. As we get closer to God, we will find ourselves wanting to do what pleases Him. Obeying God can actually be very simple. If our aim is to love Him and to love the people He's created, we won't wander far from what He wants of us.

 Pray

Father God, help me to love You and Your people. Let my life show that I love You and want to do things Your way. Amen.

HOT TOPIC | OBEDIENCE 1

Who cares?

 READ: AMOS 5:18–24

KEY VERSE V24

'But let justice roll on like a river, righteousness like a never-failing stream!'

It's obvious, not just from these verses but from many different passages in the Bible, that God is passionate about justice. Justice – care for the poor and marginalised – is a thread that runs the whole way through the Bible. Justice is a cornerstone of the books of the Law. When the prophets spoke God's words to Israel and Judah, they urged the people to exercise justice for those who needed it. A hallmark of Jesus' ministry was caring for the sick, the poor and the outcasts. If we truly want to obey God, our lives should be characterised by caring for the needy too.

This will probably mean slightly different things for each of us. It might mean helping out at your local homeless shelter, regularly donating money to an international development charity like Tearfund, or even taking a year out to be part of a project helping poor people in the developing world. It might just mean befriending the person who nobody else will talk to. But whatever it means for us, if we want to obey God, we have to take justice seriously.

HOT TOPIC | OBEDIENCE 1

 Pray

Ask God what He wants you to do to bring a little more of His justice into the world. Listen to what He has to say. Then obey!

Music to our ears

≡ **READ: PROVERBS 3:1–12**

KEY VERSE V6
'in all your ways submit to him, and he will make your paths straight.'

Music is wonderful. It has a powerful way of affecting our minds and emotions. Music can lift us and inspire us. It can speak to us in hard times, when we hear lyrics which remind us that we are not alone in the struggles we face. The opposite can be true too. Sometimes lyrics can be unsettling, hateful or abusive, and it's not great to fill our minds with that stuff. What about the things we watch, too? Could certain scenes or plot lines be having a negative impact on the way we think? If we want to live for God, we need to honour Him in everything, including the kinds of media we consume.

We might think it's OK to keep one or two areas of life off-limits to God, as long as we're obeying Him in everything else. The problem is, a bad decision in one area of life can have a big impact on your whole life. Drinking too much or experimenting with drugs can make a mess of our health, our finances and our faith. And it's so easy to wander away from God because of an unwise relationship. It's important to obey God in every decision we make. If we do that, He will always show us the best way.

➕ ## Challenge

Is there any area of your life that you've been trying to keep God away from? Now's the time to let Him in!

Weekend

Staying on track

READ: DEUTERONOMY 11:8–28

KEY VERSE V26
*'See, I am setting before you today
a blessing and a curse'*

A group of hikers were attempting the Three
Peaks Challenge – climbing the highest
mountains in Scotland, England and Wales
in 24 hours. They'd already managed Ben
Nevis, in the Scottish Highlands, and at 4am
they made a start on England's Scafell Pike.
Near the foot of the mountain, the path ran
along the bank of a river. They knew they
needed to cross the river using a ford, but it
was dark, and they couldn't see where they
were supposed to cross. So they kept going
along the path. It seemed like the sensible
option. They knew they were in trouble when
the path became less clear, the mountain got

steeper and they had to start scrambling on all fours. They checked the map and realised they were well off course. They'd missed the ford and made a bad decision to keep going. As a result of this, every step had taken them further from where they should have been. It left them in a huge mess and by the time they'd retraced their steps, they had no chance of completing the challenge within the time limit.

Often, we can't see the consequences of a little compromise. Making a small, selfish decision, even if it seems sensible at the time, can eventually lead us a long way from where God wants us. It puts us on the way to a lot of pain and frustration. Obeying God will bring blessings, because His way is always wisest. Going our own way, instead of God's, means that we're wandering away from the good plans He has for us. Let's include God in our life choices.

Think

Are you compromising on anything God wants you to do? Spend some time reflecting on this. If God calls anything to mind, ask for His forgiveness and His help to get back on track.

Fish supper

≡ **READ: JONAH 1:1–17**

KEY VERSE V3
'But Jonah ran away from the LORD and headed for Tarshish.'

⟶ Have you ever tried to take a cat to see the vet? Generally, when the cat sees you coming towards him with a basket, he'll work out what's going on, get scared, run in the opposite direction and disappear from view. You'll probably find him half an hour later, hiding behind the sofa. The cat is just delaying the inevitable, of course. It's only a matter of time before you find him, cram him into the basket and get him to the vet. Resistance is futile.

In these verses, we find Jonah behaving like the cat. It was absolutely clear to Jonah what God wanted him to do. But he decided that he didn't like this idea and ran away. The key verse tells us that Jonah wasn't just running away from God's plan, he was running away from God Himself! Also pretty futile, given that God would find Jonah wherever he went. We'd never behave like that, would we? Or maybe we would. We can sometimes feel like going our own way, especially when God's way looks scary. But God will never let us go, and He has a habit of accomplishing something when He's decided on it. Jonah found this out after spending three days inside a fish and being spat out onto a beach!

HOT TOPIC | OBEDIENCE |

➕ ## *Challenge*
Honesty time: has God told you to do something, which would take you outside your comfort zone? Are you obeying Him in this? If so, good for you. If not, ask for His help, take a deep breath and go for it.

And... relax!

READ: 1 SAMUEL 10:1–8

KEY VERSE V7
'do whatever your hand finds to do, for God is with you.'

Do you ever tie yourself in knots, trying to work out what God wants you to do – even in making tiny decisions? 'Hmmm... Shreddies or Weetabix for breakfast today? Or maybe God wants me to have Corn Flakes... or Coco Pops. Argh!'

Yesterday, we thought about how to respond when God's will isn't 100% clear. On the other hand, sometimes God just lets us choose what to do. God loves us enough to give us free will; the ability to make choices for ourselves. Sometimes, obeying God just means using our common sense and making a choice on our own, particularly when it's a small and insignificant decision. Fretting over what God wants us to eat for breakfast or what He wants us to wear today just isn't something He would want us to do.

Obviously we need to be careful with this idea. Our habit should be to listen to God, not to automatically do our own thing. But if we're honestly trying to obey God, we won't go far wrong. If we're open to His leading, God sometimes lets us do whatever we think is right.

Think

Is a small decision giving you a headache? Relax, use your common sense and do whatever you think is right. God is with you!

HOT TOPIC | OBEDIENCE 1

First things first

 READ: MATTHEW 6:25–34

KEY VERSE V33
'But seek first his kingdom and his righteousness, and all these things will be given to you as well.'

Life bombards us with so many things to worry about. It's easy to let worries about money, work, dating and all sorts of other stuff distract us from what really matters in life. What do you worry about? Maybe it's your future career plans, or lack of them? Maybe it's to do with family, friendships or relationships. Here's some wise advice: Put following God first. He'll take care of everything else. If we do our best to live for God, we may find that all the stuff we've been worrying about will gradually fall into place.

If we're set on obeying God, life won't always be easy – in fact, sometimes it will be hard. However, we'll have the satisfaction of knowing that we're working with someone who loves us utterly and forever, and for something good, purposeful and that will last for eternity. Above all, there's no need to worry! If we put God and His plans first, we can trust Him to take care of everything we need.

What do you worry about? Pray about these things, ask God to take care of them and resolve to follow Him, wherever He takes you.

✚ *Challenge*

What's your biggest worry right now? Write it down on a piece of paper, and tuck it in the page of your Bible that has today's verse on it. Decide that you're going to give that worry completely over to God, and don't stop praying about it until you do!

HOT TOPIC | OBEDIENCE 1

THURS 22 OCT

DISCIPLESHIP

Lifestyle choices
READ: PHILIPPIANS 1:27–28

KEY VERSE V27
'conduct yourselves in a manner worthy of the gospel of Christ.'

Welcome back to our study on discipleship and tips on living for Jesus.

To honour someone means to treat them with special attention and respect. We are familiar with the concept in relation to the fifth commandment to honour our mother and father. Just like with caring parents or carers, we honour God by listening to Him, taking into consideration His values, not letting Him down by behaving inappropriately and spending time with Him.

We can honour God in our everyday life and attitude. It's a good idea to regularly think about how we can reflect our relationship with Him in what we do.

So, if you play football, what is your attitude like when you play? Are you a bit aggressive, a sore loser or a cocky winner? Or you do play as part of a team, giving others the opportunity to shine. If you dance, is it just to make yourself look good? Or do you dance as an act of worship to God and the abilities He has given you?

Whatever you do, it's an opportunity to honour God and point other people towards Him. Make the most of every opportunity. People around you may question why you consider Jesus in your actions. They may not understand your relationship with Him. Stand your ground, put God first and don't give in to pressure to live life as other people do.

Discipleship Tip: Find someone to talk to about the ups and downs of being a Christian. Encourage each other with what you can both do to honour God by your lifestyle, and pray together so that you can both stand firm in following Jesus.

Think

Do you realise that you have been chosen to be a citizen of heaven? Jesus has set you apart for a life designed by Him that you can live out in all its fullness – to be worthy of an eternal life in the presence of almighty God.

'Who am I?'

READ: MATTHEW 16:13–20

KEY VERSE V16
'You are the Messiah, the Son of the living God.'

How can an encounter with Jesus change a person's life? Over the next four days we are going to look at different people from the Bible and try to answer this question.

First up is Peter. Peter was a Galilean fisherman when he first met Jesus, which was a couple of years before today's passage took place. Peter had been through a lot in those years. He'd heard Jesus teach, he'd seen Jesus heal people, he'd helped Jesus feed over 5,000 people and he had even walked on water. These experiences are what enabled him to confidently answer Jesus' question: 'Who do you say I am?'

Peter answered a call to follow Jesus, and only then was he able to be a part of these things. Our understanding of Jesus takes time to develop. To begin with, we don't understand everything; it's through our experience and knowledge of Jesus that we really get to know Him. This takes time, and every so often we need to stop and be challenged about what we think and how it affects our life.

Discipleship Tip: Set yourself this objective: to know Jesus better today than you did yesterday and to know Him more tomorrow than you do today.

Think

Do you know Jesus better than you did yesterday? Ask Him to show you something about His character, and then spend a few minutes in silence, expectantly listening for Him to speak to you.

Weekend

24/25 OCT

'Shall I heal him?'

READ: MATTHEW 8:5–13

KEY VERSE V8
'Lord, I do not deserve to have you come under my roof. But just say the word, and my servant will be healed.'

The second person from the Bible who had an encounter with Jesus is the Roman officer who had an ill servant. This officer knew about authority: 'I tell this one, "Go," and he goes; and that one, "Come," and he comes.' (v9). He probably wasn't used to asking anyone for help, particularly a travelling preacher in a Roman-occupied country. He himself was under the authority of Rome and his superior officers, and he held authority over his soldiers. However, he realised that Jesus had the power and authority of the one who sent Him. Jesus was the Son of God and therefore held the authority of God.

The officer knew the signs to look for: Jesus' conduct, the way Jesus spoke, the way He treated people and the way He commanded miracles. He recognised God's power in Jesus and understood who Jesus was. He had complete faith that Jesus could heal his servant with just a word, without even coming to his house. This is particularly amazing when we realise that this officer had not spent lots of time with Jesus as Peter had done. Jesus Himself was 'amazed' and commented that He had not found anyone else with such great faith in the whole of Israel. (What do you think the disciples felt about that?!)

When we look at what Jesus said in John 14:12: 'whoever believes in me will do the works I have been doing, and they will do even greater things than these', we can see that if we follow Jesus, we have His power and authority too!

Discipleship Tip: You have great power through your faith in Jesus. Be willing to use it – pray for people and expect things to happen – great things!

 ## *Think*

Do you have faith like the Roman officer? Who could you pray for? Ask God to show His power in that person's life.

'I see the Son of Man'

READ: ACTS 7:51–60

KEY VERSE V60
'Then he fell on his knees and cried out, "Lord, do not hold this sin against them." When he had said this, he fell asleep.'

The third individual we're going to look at whose life was powerfully impacted by Jesus is Stephen, the first Christian to be killed for his faith in Jesus. In today's passage, we find him defending himself in front of the Sanhedrin (Jewish council of leaders) against the charge of blasphemy. Stephen was bold and stood up for what he believed in. He clearly told the council that their ancestors had ignored the prophets and they had murdered the 'Righteous One' – Jesus. But they covered their ears. Then as now, sometimes people don't want to hear the truth.

Stephen was utterly convinced that Jesus was the Son of God – so much so that he was willing to die declaring it. When was the last time you stood up for what you believed? It needn't be before a large group of people but, when asked about what you believe, do you actually say you are a Christian? And if people are giving you a hard time for being a Christian, how easy do you find it to forgive them?

Discipleship Tip: Being a disciple of Christ means learning to forgive others. This can be difficult, particularly if something really serious has happened, but with the help of the Holy Spirit, forgiveness is possible.

Think

Stephen made the ultimate sacrifice for what he believed. How do you think he was able to do that?

CORE THEME | DISCIPLESHIP 2

'Who are you, Lord?'

READ: ACTS 9:1–25

KEY VERSE V5
'I am Jesus, whom you are persecuting'

The final person we are going to look at is Paul. When we first meet Paul at the stoning to death of Stephen, he is called Saul. He is out to get the Christians, as he believes that they are wrong in their belief in Jesus. He takes every opportunity to throw them into prison and to stir up trouble against them; he is 'eager to kill the Lord's followers' (v1, NLT).

Here we find him travelling to Damascus when he is hit by a brilliant beam of light. He is blinded and has a conversation with Jesus over the next three days. Then Ananias, a believer in Damascus, is sent by God to pray for Saul to regain his sight and to receive the Holy Spirit. Ananias does this, and Saul goes on to be baptised and to boldly preach that Jesus is indeed the Son of God.

Paul probably had the biggest life-changing (and name-changing) encounter with Jesus. And if Jesus can turn Paul's life around, He can turn anyone's life around.

Discipleship Tip: Listen to others who are more experienced in following Jesus and be willing to open your heart as God reveals His character to you. God will never contradict what He says in the Bible.

➕ *Challenge*

Can you think someone, whether they are a friend to you or a public figure, who you'd love to see have an amazing encounter with Jesus? Why not commit to praying for them regularly? Maybe you could ask God for a chance to talk to them about Him.

CORE THEME | DISCIPLESHIP 2

So what do you believe?

READ: 1 PETER 3:8–17

KEY VERSE V15
'Always be prepared to give an answer to everyone who asks you to give the reason for the hope that you have.'

Why believe? What would it take for some of your friends to believe in Jesus? Sometimes we can have discussions with friends about Jesus being the Son of God, about Him being an historical figure and about His miracles, yet nothing seems to convince them – even historical facts. Many people are content to see Jesus as (at most) a nice guy who did some nice things. Crowds of people in Jesus' day saw Him do miracles, meet their practical needs and show real wisdom and intelligence in His answers to their questions. But still some questioned who He was.

St Francis of Assisi is known for the saying: 'Proclaim the Gospel at all times, and if necessary, use words.' By our actions people will see what we are like and will ask us questions about why we do what we do. Then we need to be ready to engage with those questions. Clever arguments are good, but it's when people can see our faith in action that they really get interested.

Discipleship Tip: Be ready to talk about why you are a Christian, but remember that you don't have to share everything all at once. Ask God to show you the right thing to say at the right time.

 Think

Can you tell your story of why and how you became a Christian? Try saying it out loud to yourself. As you do, ask yourself: 'Do my words line up with my actions?'

CORE THEME | DISCIPLESHIP 2

What kind of fan are you?

READ: PHILIPPIANS 1:20–24

KEY VERSE V20
'I eagerly expect and hope that I will in no way be ashamed, but will have sufficient courage so that now as always Christ will be exalted'

Football fans – they sing all the songs, wear the right clothes and spend their money on the little 'extras' associated with their favourite team. However, the real crunch comes when their loyalty is tested. When their team loses, some followers suddenly go quiet. But true fans stay loyal and keep believing in their team even if they are laughed at or ignored.

When do you struggle to be open about being a Christian? What is it that you worry will happen? Facing these fears can allow you to really experience living for Jesus.

Today's reading is from Paul's letter to the Christians in Philippi. He is struggling to decide which is better – to live for Christ or die for Christ. Not much of a choice, some might say. But here we have Paul arguing each way. In his eyes, either way he is a winner. In death, he will be with Christ; and in life, he gets to tell more people about Christ. Perhaps as we get closer to God, we realise that we can trust Him in any circumstances – and we find that we're then bolder in living for Him.

Discipleship Tip: Live for Christ boldly, so that you can tell others about Him and live your life in a way that honours Him.

Pray

Tell God honestly why you sometimes struggle to be a Christian. Ask Him to help you to trust Him more, to overcome your struggles and to be strong enough to represent Jesus at all times.

CORE THEME | DISCIPLESHIP 2

Stretch yourself

READ: 1 THESSALONIANS 4:1–2

KEY VERSE V1
'live in order to please God... do this more and more.'

With the distractions and demands of day-to-day life, it can be easy to let Jesus slip down the priority list. A lot of our routine is formed around habits, and if we don't block out regular time to spend with God, weeks can suddenly fly by without us even picking up a Bible. It might be that we remember Him on Sundays, but He doesn't get much of a look-in the rest of the week.

Challenge yourself and remember: God loves to see you living a life for Him; He delights in watching you stand up for Him. To survive the challenges of being a Christian, don't settle for the good, but stretch yourself for the great. When we live for God, we are not doing so just to keep Him happy, we are fulfilling our created design. We are achieving our potential.

No matter how much of Jesus you have in your life, He has more to offer you. Keep asking Him for more, and keep on doing the things He has planned for your life. Jesus wants to walk with you every step of your journey through life. He want to be with you in the big and small moments of life today, tomorrow and forever.

Discipleship Tip: Be encouraged to keep going. Put Jesus at the centre of what you do every day.

 Pray
Ask God to equip you for the journey ahead with Him.

Weekend

31 OCT/1 NOV

Optima tenete
READ: 1 TIMOTHY 1:18–20

KEY VERSE V19
'holding on to faith and a good conscience'

What work do you do each day? Do you work or study hard? Do you apply yourself to the jobs ahead of you every day?

Timothy had a vital job ahead of him. He had been given the task of leading a church. This was a very important role and he had been entrusted with it, despite being quite young. Paul gave him all sorts of advice on the practical daily tasks he would have to fulfil. However, in the middle of all this practical advice, Paul tells Timothy the crucial ingredient in working for God: 'Cling tightly to your faith. Keep your actions clean and your conscience clear.' This advice for Timothy is good advice for us today. It is easy to get distracted by unhelpful ideas and self-centred attitudes so we need to regularly focus on what the Bible says about how to behave. With the Holy Spirit's help, we can remember what to do or say in certain situations. This is especially vital if we have got a particular job to do as Timothy did.

Paul and Timothy had a close relationship and often wrote to each other. Paul's advice for Timothy was simply to trust in Jesus first. In the first section on discipleship, we considered mentoring. If you haven't yet got someone to talk to, think about it again and see if you could ask someone you know and trust to become your mentor.

PS – if you are wondering what *optima tenete* means: it is Latin for 'Hold on to the best things in life.' Why not impress someone by dropping this phrase into a conversation!

Discipleship Tip: If we stay close to Jesus in our work, we can serve Him in *everything* we do.

Pray

Father, thank You for all You have done for me. Help me to keep close to You in everything I do, today and all this week. Amen.

Plans

READ: NEHEMIAH 2:11–20

KEY VERSE V18
'I also told them about the gracious hand of my God on me'

Great leaders are often only recognised after they have achieved success: it's only when everyone can see what they were trying to achieve that they can be appreciated for their determination and effort.

However, most great leaders make plans for their particular vision long before anyone sees the outcome of their efforts. We see this in today's reading, where we hear from Nehemiah about the plan God has laid on his heart to rebuild the wall of Jerusalem – a plan that he later achieves. But at first, he kept this vision to himself. He needed to wait for the right moment to share God's plans with others.

As a disciple of Christ, God has plans for you. He may give those plans *only* to you. You may not understand why He has chosen you to do a certain task, but God wants to be with you in your work. He wants to equip you to serve Him in whatever you are doing. Any work – be it at school, college, university, at home or in a job – can be an opportunity to serve God.

Discipleship Tip: Great opportunities to serve God cannot always be seen, but there are small ones around us every day – let's keep our eyes open to see them.

 ## *Challenge*

How can you serve God today? If you are struggling to think of anything, ask Him to open your eyes to the opportunities around you.

30 sayings

READ: PROVERBS 22:17–29

KEY VERSE V19
'So that your trust may be in the LORD, I teach you today, even you.'

Do you like lists? There are lists for all sorts of things: 10 ways to tie shoelaces; 14 steps to eating a kumquat; 10 uses for paper towels... There are plenty more!

Today we have a list that some Bible translations head up as 'Thirty Sayings of the Wise' – good old fashioned discipleship advice from the Old Testament. (If you have time, read on into chapter 23.)

God loves a diligent worker. He doesn't respond to people who just sit around and wait all day for someone else to do all the hard work. God will honour those who work hard at the tasks they are given.

Often we may feel as if we are not being rewarded for our efforts, and we see others being rewarded, apparently for no effort at all. (Have you ever wondered why people make such a fuss over reality TV contestants who don't do very much?) Hold on to God's promise. He sees all our efforts and He will reward those who go about their work without seeking glory or praise.

Discipleship Tip: If you have been given a job, then take your reward from knowing that you are working for God.

Pray

Ask God to give you the energy and drive to try your best in your work. Ask Him to remind you each day that it is not for congratulations from others that we do good things.

Where are you right now?

READ: 1 PETER 2:4–10

KEY VERSE V9
'you are a chosen people, a royal priesthood, a holy nation, God's special possession, that you may declare the praises of him who called you out of darkness'

In thinking about the many ways in which we can live for God, an important thing to consider is why we are where we are. Where are you right now? Are you at home, at school, at college, at the shops?

Serving Jesus doesn't necessarily require travelling to the far ends of the earth and living in a tent (although it's possible God may ask you to do that in the future). You are most probably surrounded by people whose only knowledge of Jesus is the example they see in you. So wherever you are, you're in an important place. You could be a timely shoulder to lean on for a family member or a helping hand to an older person at the shops.

Where you are now, your efforts to include Jesus in everything you do are the loudest and most effective example of Christ anybody could give to those around you. God has called you out of darkness into His wonderful light and has set you as His representative – His priest – in everything you do. Your friends and your family see Jesus through you. So shine bright!

Discipleship Tip: Remember that you're God's representative. Everything you do can show more of Him to people around you.

Pray

Ask God to strengthen you to be a good example of Jesus in your work, your family and your community. Ask Him to prepare you for the conversations that may arise from your example.

CORE THEME | DISCIPLESHIP 2

THURS 5 NOV

Free gift

READ: TITUS 3:3–8

KEY VERSE V5

'he saved us, not because of righteous things we had done, but because of his mercy.'

In today's reading, Paul is writing to Titus, in Crete at the time, to encourage him to continue working with the local people even though it was hard and they were messing him around. Paul gives Titus some practical tips about how he could help the Cretans to overcome their past way of life and launch out into living brand-new Christian lives.

Have you ever made a mistake? Ever done some really good things for others? Well, God loves you no matter how many mistakes you've made or how many good deeds you've done – or any combination of the two. God's love isn't something we have to work really hard to earn – it's a free gift! And because of God's love, He has saved us from the mess of our old life and set us up clean and ready for our new life. God has dealt with our past, so we don't have to let it hold us back. God washed away our sins, giving us a new birth and new life through the Holy Spirit. He declared us not guilty because of His great kindness. And now we're free to live God's way!

Discipleship Tip: Remember that God loves you and has saved you, no matter how many good or bad things you've done. He loves us – not because we deserve it, but just because He's so good!

Pray

Thank God for the gift of His Son, Jesus. Ask Him to help you never to take that gift for granted.

Let it go

≡ **READ: COLOSSIANS 3:1–15**

KEY VERSE V13
'Forgive as the Lord forgave you.'

In his letter to the Colossian Christians, Paul outlines how to live as disciples because of the new life God has given us. He explains how to interact with others and respond to situations around us with compassion, kindness, humility, gentleness and patience – even when it's not easy.

We all have faults and it's probably easier to see them in other people than in ourselves. But just think how long it took you to learn to ride a bike, drive a car or speak another language. It took time, it took patience and it took others investing in you. It's just the same in working out your new life: it takes time to change and, believe it or not, others might need to forgive you – possibly because of something you said or did.

There might be past behaviour or actions that you are not proud of. Maybe you have taken advantage of a person's gentle nature and made fun of them. If you can, why not try to make amends and apologise. You will be modelling godly behaviour and showing humility to someone else – plus you will probably feel a weight has been lifted.

Discipleship Tip: Learn to forgive others *and* to say sorry to others for your mistakes. Both are important, and will change your life!

Think

Is there someone you are struggling to forgive at the moment? Or do you need to ask forgiveness from somebody else?

**WEEKEND
7/8 NOV**

PEER PRESSURE

Time for a refresh!

READ: ROMANS 12:1–5

KEY VERSE V2
'Do not conform to the pattern of this world, but be transformed by the renewing of your mind.'

For the next two weeks, we're back to on the theme of peer pressure. Previously we spent some time thinking about what peer pressure is and where it comes from. We've thought about what others might pressure us into doing, and how sometimes our influence can be used for positive ends. All in all, we've got a good handle on the issue. So, what next?

We would almost certainly be worried if, when we went to the doctor, the doctor told us what was wrong with us but then said nothing about a cure or a treatment. Knowing there's an obstacle to face is half the battle, but the other half is knowing how to deal with that obstacle when the time comes. So, over the next couple of weeks we're going to look at what pointers the writers of the Bible give us about how to deal with peer pressure.

Today's verse sets the scene. The apostle Paul writes to the church in Rome, telling them very clearly that the way in which they act and think should be obviously different from the actions and thoughts of the world around them. As Christians, there are some things we shouldn't be a part of: joining in with negative peer pressure is one of those things. So, how do we go about freeing ourselves from peer pressure and encourage others in this too? Let's get started!

Pray

Dear Lord, please give me the tools I need to deal with peer pressure. Increase my confidence in You and Your plan for my life. Amen.

Please keep off the grass

≡ **READ: PROVERBS 1:10–15**

KEY VERSE V15
'my son, do not go along with them, do not set foot on their paths'

→ Don't touch! I wonder how many times we've seen a similar warning. There's something about human nature that means, when we see a sign like this, our first thought is to do exactly the opposite! Many of us often find it very hard to heed a warning – no matter how loudly or clearly it's given.

Today's Bible verse tries to do just that – issue a warning, loud and clear. 'Stay away!' the writer warns. There are people who will try to lead you to do things that aren't good. This is a good place to start when thinking about how best to deal with peer pressure – steer clear!

If we know people who make a habit of dragging others into the trouble they're caught up in, it might be best to stay away from them. Now, this might be easier said than done, since often the things we ought to stay away from are the most tempting. Like the 'Don't Touch!' sign, things we know aren't good can have an unusual attraction. Sometimes we hang around with people we know will get us into trouble, but the bottom line is that they are going to drag us into things we shouldn't be doing – and we need to avoid that. Today's verse is a simple warning, but one we need to heed: 'Stay away!'

🕱 *Think*
What are you being led into that you need to steer clear of? Be honest with God and with yourself, and ask for God's help to resist.

HOT TOPIC | PEER PRESSURE 2

Let your light shine

READ: MATTHEW 5:13–16

KEY VERSE V15

'Neither do people light a lamp and put it under a bowl. Instead they put it on its stand'

Today's Bible verses might be quite well known to us. You may have heard a sermon or talk on this passage before, especially as the visual metaphors of salt and light are so relatable and memorable. But take a moment today to think about what these words might mean when it comes to peer pressure.

We are called to be like a light in the darkness. We might imagine those listening to Jesus' words about light would have laughed at how silly what He was suggesting sounded. Who in their right mind would take something as warming and reassuring as a light in a dark house and then hide it away where it was of no good to anyone?

Jesus is in us, and we can shine in a dark world. So, why would we hide ourselves away? Why not let everyone see the difference Jesus can make? Today's verses remind us that sometimes we are going to stand out – we're going to have to be the only light in a dark place. There are times when, no matter what everyone else around is doing, we're going to have to do something else. People will notice if we are brave enough not to go along with what everyone else is doing. Are you up for the challenge?

Challenge

Set yourself the challenge today to step out of your comfort zone somehow – whether it's by talking to someone about Jesus, or simply making a different choice.

HOT TOPIC | PEER PRESSURE 2

Goal-setting

☰ **READ: MATTHEW 6:19–34**

KEY VERSE V33

*'But seek first his kingdom and his righteousness,
and all these things will be given to you as well.'*

What are your priorities? Our lives are full of conflicting demands upon our time and energy. Do we prize being popular above all – or value fitting in more than anything else? What about money, fame and academic achievement: which of these do we want most?

The question of priorities is important. We only have so much time and energy – we can't do everything. So we put the most time and energy into what we see as the most important. If we want to be popular, then that is where we will devote our energies, perhaps bowing to peer pressure to make sure that we remain in favour.

If we listen to the many other social pressures in our world, we hear that money and fame are the be all and end all. We might be tempted to invest our time and resources into securing them. However, today's Bible verse gives a heavenly perspective on the question of priorities. We are told to seek God's kingdom above all else. The rewards are clear, yet so is the cost. If we make this our number one goal, then we cannot devote our time and energy to pursuing the many other goals we are being pressured to achieve. And, if we give in to peer pressure, our energies are not being used to seek the kingdom of God.

HOT TOPIC | PEER PRESSURE 2

➕ ## Challenge

Write your priorities down on a piece of paper. Then spend some time with God, asking Him what He would like you to do. Reflect on how His desires for you match up with your own.

The true test

READ: PHILIPPIANS 4:2–9

KEY VERSE V8
'Finally, brothers and sisters, whatever is true, whatever is noble, whatever is right… think about such things.'

In chemistry lessons, one of the first things you learn is how to find the pH of a chemical using litmus paper. You do this by dipping the end of the paper into a substance. After a couple of seconds, you remove the paper and compare the colour on the strip with a colour chart.

These tests help pupils to get a definite answer. Is it blue or red, alkaline or acid? Tests like this allow them to be sure whether they are right or not. Today's Bible verse introduces a different kind of indicator test. It's a test which tells us not what something's made of, but rather whether or not something is of God or not of God. These verses provide a good benchmark when we are being pressured into doing something.

Is what we're being pushed towards true, noble, right, pure, lovely, admirable, excellent or praiseworthy? If not, then it's probably something to avoid at all costs. It's not always 100% obvious whether something is true, noble, etc – and we'll look at how to deal with that in a few days' time. However, in the meantime, this can be a useful test when we're being pushed towards something. Does the test indicate it's something good or something we should avoid?

HOT TOPIC | PEER PRESSURE 2

Think

What kind of activities would you describe as not being true, noble, pure, lovely, admirable, excellent or praiseworthy? Ask God for His help to change.

Eyes on the prize

READ: HEBREWS 12:1–4

KEY VERSES VV1–2
'And let us run with perseverance the race marked out for us, fixing our eyes on Jesus'

Many of you will have taken part in a cross-country run at school. Whether through the local woods or around the school field, cross-country running is about stamina. For some, running long distances is not a problem and can even be quite good fun. But for many, the idea of running that far is not a nice one!

The first 200 metres are usually fine, then the next 200 metres may be all right, but after that it starts to get harder and harder – until it really becomes a case of mind over matter in order to finish the race. Today's Bible verse reminds us that living as a Christian can often be like this. Sometimes it's easy, but there will be times when it's tiring and draining, and it would be far easier to stop and have a sit down rather than carry on running.

When it comes to resisting peer pressure, it's also a case of endurance. It would be nice if once we'd said no that was it. However, the reality is that we have to keep on saying no; we have to continue to resist the pressure from those around us. It's going to be tiring, and it's going to be tempting to give up and give in to the pressure from those around us. But let's keep on going, because the finish line is one well worth reaching.

HOT TOPIC | PEER PRESSURE 2

🔎 Think

What do you do when resisting the peer pressure around you gets too much? Think about how you could recharge so that you can keep on running.

Weekend

14/15 NOV

Make God smile

READ: 1 THESSALONIANS 4:1–2

KEY VERSE V1
*'Finally, dear brothers and sisters, we urge
you in the name of the Lord Jesus to live in
a way that pleases God' (NLT)*

Having a really good teacher will often be
what inspires students to work hard. All they
want is to do what's right; to do what the
teacher wants and to be recognised as having
done the right thing. Hard-working students
are occasionally given a hard time by those
around them – they get labelled 'teacher's pet'
or worse. However, this name-calling often
comes from a kind of jealousy. Secretly, most
of us would quite like to be told that we've
done a good job. We like to know that we've
pleased the one in charge, and that they've
noticed. We might not admit it, but it's a good

feeling when the teacher notices that we've got it right.

Today's key verse is a request for us to please someone a bit more important than our maths teacher. It reminds us that we need to be living lives that please God – not because that's what gets us into heaven, but because why wouldn't we want to please the one who has given us so, so much?!

What's this got to do with peer pressure? Well, it gives us another tool to help us decide how to act. When thinking about whether to do what our friends want us to do – when we have to decide whether to conform or to stand out – we need to think about whether it will please God. Let's also bear in mind that when we choose to please God, it's possible (or even likely) that we're going to get called names – but it will probably be because the name-callers have noticed that we have something in our character that they want!

 ## *Pray*

Dear Lord, help me to always act in a way that will please You. Help me and guide me to make decisions that take me along paths that are good. Amen.

Copy cat

≡ **READ: PROVERBS 22:24–25**

KEY VERSES VV24–25
'Do not make friends with a hot-tempered person, do not associate with one easily angered, or you may learn their ways and get yourself ensnared.'

If you're lucky enough to have younger brothers or sisters, or have friends with younger siblings, you'll know that they are swift to learn from those around them. You have to be very careful what you say and what you do around them, because they are quick to copy – and don't always copy the right things!

However, it's not only younger children who emulate the behaviour of those around them. Our peers can often be hugely influential in persuading us how to act or what to do. Today's Bible verse adds the next helpful piece of advice. If we know someone is going to teach us the wrong things, let's not hang around with them. No matter how much we think we can resist copying their behaviour, it might just be easier not to associate with them in the first place.

This can be hard, especially when it forces us to distance ourselves from people who are popular. However, if it stops us being pressured into things we are best out of, it might be better in the long run!

⬆ *Pray*

Dear Lord, surround me with people who will build me up and will teach me to be more like Jesus. Help me to steer clear of people who will lead me into ways that take me away from You. Amen.

Getting rid of gossip

 READ: 1 PETER 3:13–17

KEY VERSE V16
'keeping a clear conscience, so that those who speak maliciously against your good behaviour in Christ may be ashamed'

Schools, churches and youth groups are all, whether we like it or not, prone to a little gossip. Something happens or someone does something, and very quickly everyone knows about it – and has said what they think about it.

Avoiding gossip is hard, and eliminating it is even harder, but today's verse gives us some helpful advice, especially when we apply it to the question of peer pressure. It reminds us of the importance of giving those around us as little fuel for gossip as possible.

People are going to talk about what you do and, if you stand up against peer pressure, they will probably talk about you all the more. However, if you've stood up for what you believe in, and you've done it with humility and gentleness rather than rubbing it in people's faces, today's verse assures us that those gossiping will soon realise that you are in the right.

Gossip can be a huge problem for groups, but if we stay strong and make sure our consciences are clear, we have nothing to worry about.

 Think

Do you gossip about others? Where and when do you find it hardest not to gossip about others?

HOT TOPIC | PEER PRESSURE 2

Oh, wise one

 **READ: JAMES 1:2–8**

KEY VERSE V5
'If any of you lacks wisdom, you should ask God, who gives generously to all without finding fault, and it will be given to you.'

All of us will know the best people to have on our team in a quiz. There are some people who are really good at knowing the right answers: they seem to have a gift for remembering things and applying what they know to the questions being asked. Others find it much harder to choose the right answer: it might be this one or it might be that one.

Every day we're faced with pressures from all sides to do all sorts of things. Sometimes it's easy to spot the times when we're better off out of it – when we need to be strong and say no. But at other times it's a lot harder to discern whether it's OK to be doing it or not. Today's Bible verse reassures us that there's something we can do when we find ourselves in this situation.

Our God is a generous God, and He wants to help us do the right thing. We are not on our own when faced with tough decisions. We can ask God for wisdom to help us know when we need to stand firm and when it's OK to go with the flow. It's wonderful to know that there's someone out there who will guide us.

 Pray
Spend some time asking God for the wisdom you need. What is it you need to know? What are you not sure about?

Kitted out

 READ: EPHESIANS 6:10–17

KEY VERSE V13
'Therefore put on the full armour of God, so that when the day of evil comes, you may be able to stand your ground'

If you've ever played any cricket or hockey, you'll know that you need an awful lot of equipment in order to take part in the game. Some of this equipment makes playing the game easier (it would be pretty hard to play cricket without a cricket bat), and some of it makes playing the game safer (anyone who's played hockey without shin pads will appreciate why they're needed!).

Today's Bible verses tell us about a different type of equipment – equipment not for playing sport but for living as a Christian. It's often referred to as the armour of God and is vital survival gear for our Christian journey.

The armour includes truth, peace, faith, salvation, God's righteousness and the Word of God – not shin pads and face guards, but far more useful when it comes to being a Christian. When facing issues such as peer pressure, if we pursue the truth, stay in a right relationship with God, seek peace, hang on to our faith, remember our salvation and use the Word of God, we'll find it easier to win the game. You shouldn't play sports without suitable equipment, so let's not start our day without the armour of God.

 Think

Which part of the equipment that God provides do you tend to lean on the most? Is there a part of the armour of God that you particularly need to 'put on' today?

HOT TOPIC | PEER PRESSURE 2

Follow the leader

READ: ROMANS 6:15–18

KEY VERSE V16
'Don't you know that when you offer yourselves to someone as obedient slaves, you are slaves of the one you obey...?'

→ We ended our first section on peer pressure thinking about choices, and that is where we finish again. Today's Bible verse gives a very clear message. We have a choice over what guides our thinking and, whatever we choose, we become a slave to it.

It sounds rather dramatic, and we might be tempted to dismiss this as over the top, but in reality it's all too true. When we give in to peer pressure, we become a slave to the ideas and actions of others. It's then possible that this slavery will end up getting us into trouble and will lead us along paths we wouldn't have chosen ourselves. However, we have another choice. We can resist the influences of those around us, no matter how fierce the pressure, and we can choose to obey God and seek His will for our lives.

God says He will help us do this by giving us wisdom, by helping us to know what is pure and what's not, by helping us to surround ourselves with people who won't pressure us into sin, and by helping us to resist the effects of the gossip and hardship that might follow. But despite all this, it comes down to a choice – who do you choose to obey?

Challenge

Who do you obey? What are you a slave to?
Challenge yourself to choose God every time!

HOT TOPIC | PEER PRESSURE 2

**WEEKEND
21/22 NOV**

HUMOUR

Holy flaws

READ: JOSHUA 2:1–11

KEY VERSES VV1–2

'Then Joshua son of Nun secretly sent two spies... So they went and entered the house of a prostitute named Rahab and stayed there.'

Ironic humour is not laugh-out-loud funny, but it is very amusing when the opposite of a situation is said or done to make a point. Perhaps the greatest irony of all is that our perfect God is head over heels for us imperfect humans and has a plan for each one of us, regardless of our flaws.

When we take a closer look at Jesus' family tree, we find all sorts of less-than-perfect characters. From the line of Rahab, a prostitute who ran an inn in Jericho and hid Joshua's spies, came Jesus, the Son of God. Rahab's family were spared when the Israelites conquered Jericho and she later went on

87

to marry a man called Salmon, who was the great-great grandfather of King David, as mentioned in Matthew 1:4–5. So Jesus' ancestor was a prostitute!

Then there was Noah, who after his tremendous act of faith in building the ark, is found a few years later rolling around naked and drunk (Gen. 9:20–23); Jacob and Rebekah deceive Isaac to gain a blessing, by pretending that Jacob is his brother Esau (Gen. 27); David, considered to be Israel's greatest ever king, went on to commit adultery and have the woman's husband killed (2 Sam. 11).

So often we feel like a failure and we begin to wonder if God can really love or use someone like us. But God delights in working through the most unlikely people. A quick scan through Jesus' family tree will tell you that (see Matt. 1). So will looking around you at church on Sunday. God just loves people – warts and all.

Pray

This kind of ironic humour gives us hope. We are just as undeserving of God's favour as the people we find in the Bible, but God's love, forgiveness and restorative power are for us, just as they were for them. Thank God that He loves you as you are and wants you to be a part of His great plans, today!

Puzzled priorities?

 READ: JONAH 4:1–11

KEY VERSE V8

'the sun blazed on Jonah's head so that he grew faint. He wanted to die, and said, "It would be better for me to die than to live."'

Satire is the use of humour to expose foolishness or injustice. It has a purpose. It uses the power of humour to change minds and influence events. It might be called the weapon of the weapon-less as it is often used by the underdog in a situation.

The book of Jonah is one of the best examples of satire in the Bible. Jonah finally makes it to Nineveh, moaning all the way, after initially being reluctant enough to run in the opposite direction. He then warns Nineveh of God's anger as he had been commanded to do, but when the people repent, God has mercy on them and Jonah starts sulking again – because God was 'too loving'. In the passage we've just read, God uses a plant to make the point that He cares about things that He makes – plants, animals and most of all, people.

God's point in verses 10–11 puts Jonah in his place. In all his self-absorbed sulking and moaning, Jonah had lost sight of the thousands of lost and helpless people who needed to hear God's message.

Think

The satirical challenge presented to Jonah is also a challenge to us. Are we caring more about our own personal circumstances and wellbeing than about the millions of people in the world who don't know the God who loves them and wants to rescue them?

HOT TOPIC | HUMOUR 2

Cultural comedy

 READ: MATTHEW 7:1–5

KEY VERSE V3
'Why do you look at the speck of sawdust in your brother's eye and pay no attention to the plank in your own eye?'

Jesus often used irony, hyperbole and ridiculous or exaggerated pictures. You've probably heard the joke about the horse with the 'long face', or the peanut that was 'assaulted'. Jesus brings us the man trying to remove the speck of sawdust from his friend's eye when he has a huge plank of wood in his own. The visual humour is there, but we often miss it because we have heard it so many times or because of the differences between our own culture and the culture of the time and place during Jesus' earthly life.

Imagine for a moment the image of this particular scenario as if it were in a slapstick comedy film: Guy #1 has a huge plank in his eye but is trying to remove a speck of sawdust from Guy #2's eye. The plank is so big that as #1 comes close to try to remove the speck from #2, the plank jabs #2 in his healthy eye. Then as #2 is recovering, #1 whips his head around at the sound of another voice and knocks #2 to the ground. And on it goes... Through this ridiculous visual picture, Jesus is making a point. His use of humour adds colour and flavour to His message and helps us to remember it.

HOT TOPIC | HUMOUR 2

 Think

The world needs more Christian stand-up comedians, satirical journalists, authors, scriptwriters, songwriters and more. What talents or influence has God given you that you can pair with humour to spread God's message?

Adventure awaits...

≡ **READ: MATTHEW 19:16–30**

KEY VERSE V24
'Again I tell you, it is easier for a camel to go through the eye of a needle than for someone who is rich to enter the kingdom of God.'

A man who has all the earthly wealth and influence he could want comes to Jesus seeking a guaranteed ticket to heaven. But he's underestimating heaven as a nice place to chill once you die. The kingdom of heaven is so much more than that.

The kingdom of heaven is here and now in us, as well as in eternity. It's about relationships and adventure and growth; quests and missions; fighting the good fight; taking back ground and souls from the devil and bringing them back into the joy, freedom and glory of God!

We often use humour to help us cope with sorrow. It wasn't just the young man who went away sad, but Jesus' heart ached for him too. His satirical camel-and-needle analogy showed that the man's earthly security was actually his downfall. He was not willing to give up comfort and predictability on earth in exchange for a life of adventure and purpose, even with the promise of even greater reward in heaven.

Consider this: the inspirational books and films we love the most tend not to be about the lives of those who 'played it safe', but on those who risked it all and gave everything for something bigger than themselves.

HOT TOPIC | HUMOUR 2

⬆ *Pray*
Is there something you are reluctant to give up – perhaps an unhelpful influence in your life or an unhealthy habit? Pray that God will help you let go of it and trust that He will give you far better in exchange.

Life of the party

READ: LUKE 19:1-10

KEY VERSE V7
'All the people saw this and began to mutter, "He has gone to be the guest of a sinner."'

Jesus loved a good party! He was actually renowned for it, laughing and dining with tax collectors like Zaccheus and Matthew/Levi (Matt. 9:10; Luke 15), women with a reputation (Luke 7:39) and other notorious sinners.

These were people who, for whatever reason, found themselves at a place in life where people scorned them and looked down at them as if they were trash. But they were drawn to Jesus because He saw beyond the poor choices, the abuse and the other circumstances that had shaped their lives, and saw the lost and precious child inside them. Jesus never condoned lawlessness or impure living, but he knew these people yearned for a new and better way, so they followed Him. He could work with that.

He loved them as they were: He welcomed them, embraced them and offered a safe space to have fun in, unjudged and joyful. When we know that we have a certain reputation, we tend to accept it and behave in a way that perpetuates that reputation. The key to breaking the cycle is realising that we are not our past. We get to make fresh decisions every day. And the strength to do that comes from knowing that we are loved, valued and included.

Think

Is there someone you know who tends to be left out, ostracised because they are different? How does Jesus see them? Think how you can reach out and include them... then go do it.

HOT TOPIC | HUMOUR 2

Riff off!

 READ: MARK 7:24–30

KEY VERSE V27
'First let the children eat all they want… for it is not right to take the children's bread and toss it to the dogs.'

This passage is a puzzling bit of banter. A woman comes to Jesus, begging Him to heal her little daughter who is being tortured by a demonic spirit. Jesus then seems to say that He cannot heal her daughter because she is a dog.

Taken at its face value, Jesus' comment is rude, insulting and heartless. How can we possibly accept such a picture of Christ? The woman responds, however, with a witty retort, that even dogs can eat the crumbs that fall from the table. Jesus then immediately tells her that He has healed her daughter. This is a strange account indeed. But beneath the comedy lay the woman's love for her daughter and her faith – which Jesus was testing, and found to be true. Humour is exchanged here but through it, serious issues are addressed, and Jesus responds with admiration for a 'worthy opponent' (who was loved all along), and a miracle.

Humour is a way to express serious things. Laughter relaxes people. The jokes (when timed appropriately and with good intentions) can raise issues that may not be raised anywhere else and if it can be joked about, it can be talked about.

 ## Challenge

Sometimes when a friend is going through a tough time, it can be hard to know how to respond. But joy and faith-filled prayer are a dynamic duo. Don't be afraid to bring both of them into someone's hard situation.

HOT TOPIC | HUMOUR 2

Weekend

28/29 NOV

Diffusing the situation

READ: LUKE 15:1–7

≡ KEY VERSES VV1–2

'Now the tax collectors and sinners were all gathering round to hear Jesus. But the Pharisees and the teachers of the law muttered, "This man welcomes sinners, and eats with them."'

Jesus is at it again, partying the day away with society's 'unfavourables'. And the Pharisees are at it again too, wagging their perfectly manicured beards in disdain. By this point, they're itching for a fight. But God invented the use of humour to diffuse a conflict situation. So Jesus pulls out His next party trick, called parody.

When Jesus hears their snide comments, instead of rising to the bait He tells stories – and humorous ones at that! Who in their right mind would leave their 99 sheep to go and hunt for one missing one? Jesus would, but at first glance it seems absurd.

And actually it *is* absurd! But when we look closer, Jesus is telling a parody of Himself – of how completely irrational yet utterly unconditional His love and care for us is. Jesus doesn't mind being the butt of the joke – He's got the sense of humour and the security in His identity to handle it, and it confounds the serious Pharisees.

We have to be able to laugh at ourselves. It's a gift! And it can diffuse a conflict before it really gets started. Sometimes the best thing is to lighten the situation, maybe with a well-placed joke or a story. At other times the wisest thing to do in a tense situation is to avoid the conflict while it is heated. Perhaps you just need to let it go altogether, or maybe it does need to be addressed – but later, after the tension has eased.

Challenge

Next time you see conflict arising, try to lighten the situation with a joke. Or if you're in a disagreement with someone, resist the temptation to fuel the fire. Instead, take a breath and let it go, or come back to it later when the heat has gone out of the moment.

Be the exception

READ: MARK 10:35–45

KEY VERSE V45

'For even the Son of Man did not come to be served, but to serve, and to give his life as a ransom for many.'

HOT TOPIC | HUMOUR 2

A lot of jokes are to do with broken rules and surprising meanings. The build-up of a joke leads you to expect a certain outcome, and then the punchline overturns your expectations. Jesus Himself was bit of an enigma at times. In everything He did, He overturned expectations. People expected a king on a powerful horse, and He arrived in Jerusalem on a donkey. People expected a warrior and He came to bring peace. People expected a ruler and Jesus came as a servant.

In a world that says we need to make money and own a nice car and a big house to be successful, Jesus calls us to follow His example and live lives of incongruity. In a world where it's apparently acceptable to put others down to make ourselves look better and climb over others to get up the career ladder, we are called to live humbly and to serve others. In a world that encourages us to get as much as we can, Jesus urges us to give. The challenge for us is to be the punchline (for now); to be the opposite of the egocentric world around us; to be servant-hearted, generous, humble, and to love our enemies. God-given honour, wealth, glory – all will come to God's faithful ones, in His way and in His timing.

Think

'So the last will be first, and the first will be last' (Matt. 20:16). Reflect on those words. How might they affect your attitudes and lifestyle?

Living with eternity in mind

≡ **READ: ACTS 2:14–36**

KEY VERSE V24
'But God raised him from the dead, freeing him from the agony of death, because it was impossible for death to keep its hold on him.'

→ Of course, the greatest incongruity of Jesus' life is in death; in the cross and resurrection. People's expectations were that death was the end, but Jesus turned it all on its head. He turned the whole of history upside down by coming back to life! Death could not keep Him in its grip. In some churches, Christians celebrate Holy Humour Sunday at Easter, celebrating the huge joke that God pulled on Satan by bringing Jesus back to life from death.

As Christians, we are 'Easter people' rejoicing in life after death. We should not dwell on the darkness and suffering of the cross without rejoicing in the new life available to us. When we encounter hardships, we can be happy because we know that God is with us, giving us His strength and grace. When we get sick, we can joyfully thank God that because of Jesus we are healed – and await that healing with confidence. When we are sad or lonely, we can smile knowing that the creator of all heaven and earth loves us desperately and will never leave us. We have so much to smile, laugh and rejoice about!

⬆ *Pray*
Thank God for Jesus' resurrection and the new life available to us because of it! Death has been overcome and Jesus has opened up the way for us to enter the kingdom of heaven – and for it to enter us! Ask God to help you live on earth… with eternity in mind.

HOT TOPIC | HUMOUR 2

'Good' gossiper

READ: LAMENTATIONS 3:1–24

KEY VERSE V14
'I became the laughing-stock of all my people; they mock me in song all day long.'

HOT TOPIC | HUMOUR 2

When you're having a hard time, just have a read of this passage. Lamentations is a true piece of lamenting and raw, open pain. The author is incredibly honest with God about his feelings, while still remembering God's goodness: 'His compassions never fail. They are new every morning; great is your faithfulness' (vv22–24). Lamentations, Job and the book of Psalms show us that we can be honest with God about our struggles and the things that upset us. If we want to shout at God for something, that is OK. He is big enough to cope.

In verse 14 though, the author laments his so-called friends laughing at him and even making up mocking songs about him. Some friends, eh? He is at his lowest point and even his friends let him down.

Have you ever gossiped or laughed at the expense of someone else, or not stood up for them when someone else has been making fun of them? Perhaps you've been on the receiving end of gossip or mocking. Makes you feel wretched, doesn't it? You can change the environment though – by being a 'good' gossiper, saying nice things to and about people. It makes others stop and ponder their words too.

Pray
Pray for the courage to stand up to gossiping and mocking. Pray that God will help you to notice good things about others, and that He will help you to speak up and bring joy!

Inappropriate banter

 READ: EPHESIANS 5:1–20

KEY VERSE V4
'Nor should there be obscenity, foolish talk or coarse joking, which are out of place, but rather thanksgiving.'

It's far too easy to join in when other people are making coarse, crude or offensive jokes. A rude, racist, sexist or homophobic joke might make us feel part of the crowd if we laugh, or look a bit edgy if we repeat it, but Paul is very clear that this kind of behaviour is not for us.

Writing to the Ephesians, he spells out that this kind of humour is not fitting for us as Christians. And we don't even need it! God created us to smile, to laugh, to find joy in every day – and in creating us for these things He has also given us the character, the cleverness and the tools to be able to make up good, clean, happy jokes that don't bring pain or sorrow to anyone.

As we have already seen, humour is often about opposites. Paul encourages us to think and talk in an 'opposite' manner. Instead of sharing crude jokes and off-colour comments, he encourages us to give thanks. Why? Because when we give thanks, we focus on God. When we focus on God, He can lead us to find laughter and fun in ways that are life-affirming, positive, generous, kind and inclusive.

HOT TOPIC | HUMOUR 2

 ## *Think*

Do you worry about what other people will think of you if you do not laugh at or join in with gutter humour? Turn your mind instead to what God thinks, and ask Him to help you to think with His kind of humour.

Your morning mantra

READ: PHILIPPIANS 4:1–9

KEY VERSE V8
'whatever is true... noble... right... pure... lovely... admirable... excellent or praiseworthy – think about such things.'

→ Think how much joy is found when the traits listed in today's key verse are present. When truth is spoken instead of lies. When honour is given instead of dishonour. When right triumphs over wrong. When things are pure instead of sordid. Lovely instead of unkind. Admirable instead of degrading. Excellent or praiseworthy instead of half-hearted or embarrassing.

Jesus emanated all these things while living real life – everyday life like ours: walking, talking, eating, partying, making new friends from different social circles all along the way. No one was excluded, no one was told they were 'not enough'. He looked for the best in people, and He found it. And people loved being around Him so much that crowds followed Him everywhere He went. That doesn't sound like a boring guy.

We already looked at this passage from Philippians when thinking about peer pressure, but it's also a good rule of thumb for how we use humour. You might like to use it as a mantra when you get out of bed and start the day. It's a good target to aim for in your thoughts, words and actions. It will also make life more fun as you bring joy and laughter to those in your world!

 ## *Challenge*
Honour God with everything you are, including your sense of humour. Keep asking Him to reveal His sense of fun and humour to you, and through you.

HOT TOPIC | HUMOUR 2

OBEDIENCE

Sound advice

READ: EPHESIANS 5:15–33

KEY VERSE V21
'Submit to one another out of reverence for Christ.'

In part one, we unpacked what it means to obey God. We now move on to discuss obeying other people. It's important to know who to obey. When we are little, our parents tell us not to play with matches and fire. If we hadn't obeyed, we could have ended up with some nasty burns. On the other hand, some people will try to influence you to drink too much, take drugs or steal from shops. If you blindly obey them, you can end up in a real mess. So who should we obey, and why? Over the next couple of weeks we'll discuss what obedience looks like. We'll also look at what we should do if obeying another person would compromise our obedience to God.

The first good reason for obeying other people is that this is an important part of obeying God. In today's reading, Paul urges us that submitting to God should lead us to submit to one another. We should be humble enough to put other people first, rather than insisting on getting our own way. Submitting to people can feel uncomfortable, just as submitting to God can. But Paul is not insisting that we behave like a doormat for anyone who wants to take advantage of us. The key is that submission and love go hand in hand. God's ideal is that we should submit to each other and love the people who have submitted to us. Submitting to someone makes us vulnerable, but we can feel secure in this if we know that the person loves us.

So, whatever happens, let's serve people around us, but if they show us no love or respect we don't have to let them walk all over us. In turn, think about who's serving you. Are you showing them love?

Think

How willing are you to submit to people? Do you need to make any changes to how you show your obedience to God through others?

Follow the leader?

READ: HEBREWS 13:7–17

KEY VERSE V17
'Have confidence in your leaders and submit to their authority'

It was a fairly dull meeting at a church. The members were discussing routine and unexciting things, but the meeting suddenly got livelier when someone questioned a decision the church leader had made. If the person had calmly questioned the decision it wouldn't have been remarkable, but he vehemently tore into the pastor, criticising him for acting without the committee's approval. It seemed that he was happy for the minister to lead the church and make decisions until he actually led the church and made decisions!

We might not always feel like obeying our spiritual leaders. They might make unpopular decisions or ask us to do things we don't feel like doing, but leadership means making decisions, and decisions don't always make a leader popular. It's OK to ask our church leaders and youth leaders questions when we don't understand what they're doing, but let's always be respectful in the way we question them, and in our response to their answers. And it's always fine to examine things they say and check that they line up with Scripture.

HOT TOPIC | OBEDIENCE 2

Pray

Ask for God's blessing on your church leaders. Ask that He will give them wisdom in their decisions and help the whole church, including you, to submit to their leadership when it's in line with God's leadership.

Respect!

READ: EPHESIANS 6:5–9

KEY VERSE V5
'Slaves, obey your earthly masters with respect and fear, and with sincerity of heart, just as you would obey Christ.'

How do you treat your teachers – or your boss? Some teachers and bosses are easy to respect, and some... not so much! Some teachers are given a really hard time by their students. This is out of order, of course. Nobody deserves to be treated like that.

The challenge for us is to show deep respect for anyone in authority over us, whether we think they deserve it or not. Obeying God should be reflected in the way we treat people, and the respect we show to our bosses and teachers is a very powerful way for our lifestyle to reflect God's truth. Perhaps it would help to imagine Jesus with you as you stack the shelves, deliver the papers or do your course work. What would He have to say about your attitude? We might not be slaves these days, but it is still important that we respect and honour people in authority over us.

Having respect for those in charge, whether we agree with them or not, is something other people take notice of. Is everyone gossiping and complaining about an authority figure in your life? Don't join in. Decide to pray for them instead.

 ## Challenge

Think of at least one person in authority over you whom you struggle to respect. When you next see or speak to them, choose to speak and act in a way that respects this person.

HOT TOPIC | OBEDIENCE 2

A command and a promise

≡ **READ: DEUTERONOMY 5:1–21**

KEY VERSE V16
'Honour your father and your mother, as the LORD your God has commanded you'

This may not be the most popular rule in the Bible, but it really is important to respect our parents. Honouring (and obeying) our parents won't always be easy. There will probably be times when we feel misunderstood or unfairly treated. Of course, we can express our opinions but, even when we disagree with our parents, we should still respect them and their point of view.

Occasionally, we are justified in disagreeing with our parents and doing what we think is right, but unless there are extreme circumstances, these occasions should be rare. Our habit should be to obey them. And when we do disagree with mum and dad, let's do so in a way that still honours and respects them.

The commandment to honour our parents comes with a promise: that it will bring a blessing to us (Deut. 5:16; Exod. 20:12). God doesn't tell us to obey our parents just to give us more rules to follow; He knows that this way genuinely is best for us.

🔎 **Think**

When are you most tempted not to obey your parents? Are you ever justified in this? How can you handle disagreements with your parents positively?

HOT TOPIC | OBEDIENCE 2

Loyal side-kick

READ: 1 SAMUEL 14:1–23

KEY VERSE V7

'"Do all that you have in mind," his armour-bearer said. "Go ahead; I am with you heart and soul."'

Rally drivers can seem pretty reckless: they swing their cars along narrow, winding roads, with seemingly no thought for the potential of instant death if they misjudge a corner. But the real hero is the co-driver; the person who sits in the passenger seat, ignores the lethal danger they face and calmly gives the driver instructions for the next turn. The co-driver has to trust the driver completely. One false move from the driver and they both could end up in hospital – or worse. But the co-driver still does their job and shows unwavering loyalty to their driver.

Respect and obedience are strongly linked to loyalty. Jonathan's idea to attack a Philistine outpost probably seemed crazy, but the armour-bearer stuck with him. He chose to trust Jonathan, stay loyal to him and obey him. The result was an incredible victory. How willing are you to stick with someone in a difficult situation? If you only obey someone when it's easy, that's not real obedience. If you trust someone fully, and a relationship has grown and developed based on mutual trust and respect, then staying loyal when life gets hard is much easier to do. Amazing things can happen if we're willing to do that.

Think

Who do you trust? How far would your loyalty to this person stretch? Pray that God would give you courage and stickability when life gets tough.

When nobody's watching

≡ **READ: GENESIS 39:1–12**

KEY VERSE V6
*'So Potiphar left everything he had in Joseph's care;
with Joseph in charge'*

Respect, loyalty and obedience require you to act with integrity – even when no one is looking! Don't be surprised when your obedience to someone prompts them to give you big opportunities and big responsibilities. Of course, you may also face the temptation to abuse the position you're in.

Joseph's obedience to Potiphar led to responsibility for everything Potiphar owned. It also led to an opportunity to sleep with Potiphar's wife. Quite possibly, he could have done it and got away with it. But Joseph had too much integrity for that. He knew that Potiphar trusted him completely and that obeying Potiphar meant honouring the trust his boss had shown him. For Joseph, obedience meant respecting Potiphar when his back was turned, not just when he was watching.

What tempts us might be different from what tempted Joseph, but the challenge for us is the same: true obedience – godly obedience – means respecting someone, whether they're watching you or not.

HOT TOPIC | OBEDIENCE 2

➕ *Challenge*

How much respect do you show people when their backs are turned? Do you find yourself grumbling, gossiping and taking advantage of them? Do you need to make any changes here?

Weekend

12/13 DEC

Serving and influencing

READ: DANIEL 2:1–19

KEY VERSE V19
'During the night the mystery was revealed to Daniel in a vision. Then Daniel praised the God of heaven'

Billy Graham was best known as an evangelist and Christian leader, but he also spent time with no fewer than 12 presidents of the United States. He was a particularly close adviser to Richard Nixon, regularly leading private church services at the White House during Nixon's presidency, and offering him guidance at the height of the Watergate scandal. Billy had a huge influence on some of the most powerful men in the world, and was hailed by one former president as 'America's pastor'. Billy's obedience to God and his faithful serving of people in power presented him with a position of real influence. Billy used this position to bring God's wisdom into hard and vitally important situations. This did not always mean agreeing with the presidents he served, but it did always mean respecting them and speaking God's truth.

Daniel's experience was similar. Simply through doing his best to serve God and serve the king, he found himself in a position of influence he would never have expected. Billy and Daniel both found that if we're willing to obey God, and loyally and respectfully serve the people in authority over us, we may get some surprising opportunities to share God's truth with powerful people. We won't all have the chance to advise world leaders, as Daniel and Billy Graham did. But obedience to God can make us more open to His wisdom, which often means that we receive insights other people won't have thought of. Showing respect and a servant attitude to powerful people can give us opportunities to share these insights with them.

 ## Pray

Lord God, thank You for being the source of all wisdom. As I try to obey You and serve people in authority, please help me to share Your wisdom with them. Amen.

Who put them in charge?

≡ **READ: ROMANS 13:1–7**

KEY VERSE V1

'Let everyone be subject to the governing authorities, for there is no authority except that which God has established.'

Obeying people in authority over us includes obeying the government. Hmmm. Does that mean we should never object or protest or hold the government accountable for what they do? Certainly not. We'll think about this a little more over the next few days but, in the meantime, let's remember that our usual response should be to submit to our government.

Paul, writing in Romans, tells us that our leaders are in power because God put them there. Before you start mentioning Hitler, Stalin and Mugabe, these guys are very extreme examples of bad leadership. The majority of national leaders do a great job, work tirelessly and have their people's best interests at heart. So our default setting should be to obey them. Of course there are exceptions. Of course there will be times when we disagree with our leaders. But, more often than not, our responsibility is to obey, keep to the law and, yes, pay our taxes!

➕ *Challenge*

God wants us to submit to our government. This means keeping to the law. Are you compromising on this at all – perhaps you download music illegally? Resolve to stick to the whole law, not just the bits you like. The only exception to this is when the law requires you to compromise your faith, and this is a very rare thing.

HOT TOPIC | OBEDIENCE 2

I owe you one!

READ: MATTHEW 22:15–22

KEY VERSE V21
'So give back to Caesar what is Caesar's, and to God what is God's.'

We owe different things to different people. We may owe the bank because of a loan they gave us to buy a car. We may owe our boss about 38 hours' work per week. We may owe our friends a few favours for all the times they've helped us with school work or given us a lift. But what do I owe the government?

This was what the Pharisees' disciples asked Jesus. They were trying to trap Jesus into either breaking the Roman law or upsetting the Jewish crowd. Jesus' answer is wonderful. He makes it clear that it is possible to obey our government while also obeying God. However, He also makes it clear that there are limits to the government's authority over us. For the Romans, the emperor was a god. Full obedience to him meant not just loyalty and paying taxes; it meant worshipping him.

Jesus' point is that a government deserves what belongs to them, but so does God. Our government have a right to ask for taxes, but only God can ask for our souls. We should obey our government, but our ultimate obedience and ultimate loyalty should be God's and God's alone.

HOT TOPIC | OBEDIENCE 2

Pray
Commit yourself to obey God above anyone else. Ask for His wisdom in how far your obedience to other people should go.

Honesty is the best policy

READ: PROVERBS 16:10–16

KEY VERSE V13
'Kings take pleasure in honest lips; they value the one who speaks what is right.'

Wise rulers value honesty. So let's speak up when there's something wrong. A leader needs wise, humble but godly, advice. We can influence our leaders in this way. If you see something that goes against God's will, speak up. Obeying our government doesn't mean just going with the flow.

In ancient Israel, the prophet and the king worked in partnership. The king's role was to lead; the prophet's role was to advise him and bring God's perspective to his decisions. That sometimes meant being outspoken or bringing a message that was hard for the king to hear. For example, Nathan encouraged David that God's blessing would always be on his family (2 Sam. 7), but later challenged and rebuked him, after David had committed adultery (2 Sam. 12). Good kings valued the prophets' perspective, even if it wasn't what they wanted to hear. Later prophets, though, brought such strident challenges to their kings that they ended up imprisoned, beaten or even killed.

We can have a prophetic role too, speaking God's truth to our leaders, respectfully protesting if God's will seems to be compromised. Fortunately, for many of us, we're unlikely to end up in prison for doing this!

HOT TOPIC | OBEDIENCE 2

Think

What might God say about what your leaders are doing? Pray about this and don't be afraid to encourage or challenge them as appropriate.

Take a step back

 READ: ROMANS 12:14–21

KEY VERSE V19
'Do not take revenge, my dear friends, but leave room for God's wrath'

Someone jostles you in a school corridor, so you push them back. They push you harder, so you hit them. Then they hit you. And so it continues. Before you know it, it's an all-out fight. Or maybe a friend makes a careless comment about you. You get upset and say something worse about them. Then they get angry and give you a mouthful of abuse. You give a mouthful back. An icy silence follows and you start avoiding each other. In either case, our instinct to take revenge makes the conflict worse.

Perhaps God insists that only He should take revenge because only He really knows what someone who hurt us was thinking, and only He can be trusted to judge people completely fairly. If someone in authority makes life hard for us, we still shouldn't take revenge, even if they seem to be going against God. We can speak up, we can protest, but if we aim to take revenge it does our cause and God's cause no good at all. The American Civil Rights Movement in the 1950s and 1960s was renowned for protesting about racial inequality powerfully, but peacefully and prayerfully. If we're treated unfairly, we can do the same, but only God should take revenge on the people who persecute us.

HOT TOPIC | OBEDIENCE 2

 Pray

Pray for the people who make your life difficult. Even if you sometimes feel you would like to see them suffer, ask God to bless them and help you through the difficulty.

Stand up and be counted

READ: ACTS 4:1–22

KEY VERSE V20
'As for us, we cannot help speaking about what we have seen and heard.'

Some years ago now, more than 3,000 Christians were driven from their homes in Ethiopia when Muslim extremists set fire to churches and houses. In the same month, a man from Bangladesh was sentenced to a year in prison for selling Christian books, and two Christian men were killed outside a church in Pakistan. This is real persecution.

Peter and John's circumstances were just as extreme. They knew that they could be imprisoned or worse for following Jesus. (In fact, of Jesus' 12 original disciples, all but Judas later faced severe persecution and almost all were executed for their faith.) But Peter and John responded to this danger with courage and determination. They resolved to speak out for God, whatever the opposition, and they told the ruling council exactly that!

In comparison to the persecution that the first disciples suffered (and which our Christian brothers and sisters around the world still suffer), we have it easy. Yes, we might encounter opposition because of what we believe, but nowhere near this extreme. So let's speak God's truth boldly! And if anyone challenges us, let's tell them clearly that we will obey God, not them.

HOT TOPIC | OBEDIENCE 2

 ## *Challenge*

Let's do what Peter and John did and tell the people around us what God has done for us. If that seems intimidating, let's pray for courage, strength and protection.

WEEKEND 19/20 DEC

DISCIPLESHIP

We are ambassadors

READ: 2 CORINTHIANS 5:14–21

KEY VERSE V20

'We are therefore Christ's ambassadors, as though God were making his appeal through us. We implore you on Christ's behalf: be reconciled to God.'

We have reached the last section on discipleship and tips for living for Jesus. Today we are looking at what it means to be an ambassador for Christ. First, what is an ambassador? It's an important official who lives in a foreign country and represents his or her own country's interests there. For example, Dame Karen Pierce was appointed as Her Majesty's Ambassador to the United States of America earlier this year. She is the first female UK ambassador to the US and her job is to represent the queen and further good relationships between the two nations.

Being an ambassador is more than fancy dinners and dressing up in posh outfits, it requires being aware of your role *all* the time; knowing what message to convey and knowing how best to behave so that you give the right impression of your employer. This can be extremely difficult sometimes if the people you are with are not interested in what you have to say.

God wants us to be ambassadors for Him. He wants us to represent Him in our school, college or work place. The people we have contact with may not know God yet but they do know us. So let's behave like representatives of the King and tell others the most important message of all: He loves everyone. As Christ's ambassadors, we might be the key person that helps someone begin a close relationship with Him.

Discipleship Tip: Every morning, get up and say: 'I am an ambassador of Christ.' And be confident that He is with you, helping you when you speak.

Challenge

It takes effort to remember that God wants to use us every day to tell others about Him. Not in a false way, but in a living way: the way in which we live our lives.

Fellowship of the Bible

READ: HEBREWS 10:19–25

KEY VERSE V25
'not giving up meeting together, as some are in the habit of doing, but encouraging one another'

How often do you get together with other Christian friends? Is it just at church on a Sunday or a mid-week group? Do you meet up apart from at organised events?

Jesus taught His disciples to meet together, to share meals together and to lovingly question each other. It is the same with us now. Jesus loves us to meet up with other Christians. Although He has called us to tell those who don't know Him about our lives with Him, He also loves it when we meet together with other Christians.

This 'fellowship' is an important part of our lives with Jesus. It's really helpful to hang out with others who have the same joys and trials of being a Christian. Now that Christmas is only just around the corner, why don't you arrange to meet up with some friends just to have fun. You could watch a Christmassy film and have popcorn, or just chat while playing a board game. Remember to invite God to be with you.

Discipleship Tip: Christmas is a great time to tell others about Jesus so when you next meet up with your Christian mates, why not take a friend with you? Be yourself and they will soon see that being a Christian isn't weird!

Pray
Father, thank You for my Christian friends. Please help me to support and encourage them. Challenge me to invite all my friends to mix together and to remember to invite You into those times too. Amen.

CORE THEME | DISCIPLESHIP 3

#BeKind

READ: GALATIANS 5:22–26

KEY VERSE V25
'Since we live by the Spirit, let us keep in step with the Spirit.'

When it comes to fruit trees, how do we tell what type of tree we are looking at? One way is by the fruit it produces – an apple tree does not produce bananas. It's exactly the same with our behaviour: how we speak and act is a reflection of what we are really like; what kind of a person we are. If we're rooted in God, we produce good fruit. God sent a helper and encourager to help us develop fruit such as love, joy, peace, kindness. Most people like to be on the receiving end of kindness. The #BeKind campaign, launched by the TV programme *This Morning*, encourages to do just that – be kind. Presenter Holly Willoughby said: 'How much better would the world be if everyone was just that bit kinder to each other?' She is echoing an important Christian principal to be loving and kind. When we don't show these traits, people around us will not know what Jesus is like because He is the ultimate example of love.

As a disciple of Christ, are you living every day letting the Holy Spirit lead you? Do your words and actions show this?

Discipleship Tip: Remember this – 'the Holy Spirit produces this kind of fruit in our lives: love, joy, peace, patience, kindness, goodness, faithfulness, gentleness, and self-control' (Gal. 5:22–23, NLT).

Think

What will you be remembered for? What fruit do you show? Are you allowing the Holy Spirit to do His work in your life?

CORE THEME | DISCIPLESHIP 3

He'll be there

READ: MATTHEW 28:18–20

KEY VERSE V20
'teaching them to obey everything I have commanded you. And surely I am with you always'

How and why are we called to be disciples? Through Jesus' final words to His followers we are now starting to understand that God loves us. Jesus has authority over all things and we can experience this love and authority through knowing Jesus.

In today's reading, we find Jesus about to go back to heaven. The disciples are probably worried and uncertain about what will happen next. But Jesus knows every detail: the Holy Spirit will come and thousands of people will start to follow Him. He knows how each of the disciples will react to this and the roles they will play. And He reassures them: 'I am with you always.'

Jesus also knows how you are going to react to situations in your life and He reassures you: 'I am with you always.' Wherever you are today, Jesus is with you and wants to be involved. This could either be really scary: 'Jesus is watching!' Or really comforting: 'Jesus is with you.' Subtle difference! Jesus is not like a spectator judging how you are doing, but a friend who knows you and wants to help you.

Discipleship Tip: Jesus is there to help – remember to ask Him.

Pray

Father, please help me to understand that You want to be involved in my life – not to tell me where I'm going wrong but to show me where I can go right. Thank You for always being there for me. Amen.

CORE THEME | DISCIPLESHIP 3

119

Left in good hands

READ: JOHN 17:11–15

KEY VERSE VV11–12
*'Holy Father, protect them by the power of your name…
While I was with them, I protected them and kept
them safe'*

It is great to be with friends and family at Christmas time. But sometimes we are not able to be with them: they may live far away or we may have had to leave them in order to travel back home. This is especially difficult if they are going through tough times. It is good to know that God is with them when we can't be and that He was looking after them.

When Jesus knew He was about to leave His disciples – His closest friends – it must have been incredibly hard for Him. As He prays, He asks God to look after the disciples, to keep them safe and care for them. Jesus and God the Father were arranging things the way we know them today. The Father keeps us safe and cares for us; Jesus is in the middle, talking to the Father on our behalf; and the Holy Spirit helps us to live God's way. We are under God's protection in the world and protected by His name until we come home to Him – when we will be with Him for eternity.

Discipleship Tip: Jesus is with us and has asked for Father God's protection over our lives. That's so comforting! Live every day with that in mind.

Think

This Christmas, think about what knowing God means to you. Is there anyone in particular who you think may need God's love this week?

The gift of Jesus

READ: JOHN 17:16–20

KEY VERSE V20
'My prayer is not for them alone. I pray also for those who will believe in me through their message'

What does today's key verse mean for each one of us? Jesus is initially praying for His closest friends – the disciples. But then He prays for 'those who will believe in me'. That's everyone who has become a Christian since then. Isn't it good to know that we have been prayed for by Jesus? But this reading also reminds us that we have to tell other people about God. In Jesus' 'Great Commission' we are told to 'go and make disciples of all nations, baptising them in the name of the Father and of the Son and of the Holy Spirit' (see Matt. 28:18–20). Think about it. One of the reasons we know about Jesus is because of others telling *us* about Him through their testimony: their story of how they met Him. Here Jesus is praying for all the people who are going to believe in Him because of what these disciples say.

This means two things: one – Jesus is praying directly for you, just as He was 2,000 years ago; two – He is praying for all those people you talk to and who come to know Him because of your story.

Discipleship Tip: Go and tell others about Jesus! Be assured and encouraged that Jesus is talking to God about you and them.

✚ Challenge

This Christmas, remember that Jesus is praying for those who come to know Him through your story. Give the best gift of all – the good news of Jesus and His love!
Happy Christmas!

Weekend

26/27 DEC

He's worth it

READ: LUKE 14:25–35

KEY VERSE V27
'And whoever does not carry their cross and follow me cannot be my disciple.'

The Boxing Day sales will already be in full swing, but if money were no object, what would be the first thing you'd run out and buy? A nice new phone? A year's supply of top quality chocolate? A Greek island? In our heads we all have dreams in which money stops being a barrier and everything becomes possible. The reality is that good things have a cost attached to them, and great things have a greater cost to them.

A relationship with Jesus is a free one, but a costly one. Free, because grace doesn't have to be earned for our sins to be forgiven, and having our relationship with God restored is offered to us freely. However, being a disciple involves us giving things up in life. Being a Christian could cost us status, money, or even some relationships. But the rewards are always worth the cost.

In this passage, Jesus does something both shocking and surprisingly common. He turns to a large gathering of followers and challenges them. He needs to challenge them because many have got caught up in all the miracles, the free lunches and the overall hype, but they need to know that there is a real cost to following God, and it's a cost that many people turn away from.

Jesus knew that following Him would not be easy and wanted us to be aware of this. Anyone who says being a Christian is easy needs to read about the disciples, who were all martyred for their faith apart from John, who was exiled. So in this life we will face trials because of our faith, whether big or small, but life with Jesus is so worth it!

Discipleship Tip: Don't be surprised when you encounter ridicule about following Jesus, but remember He went through much worse for us.

Challenge
Be aware of the cost of following Jesus in other countries by visiting opendoorsuk.org online.

Follow His lead

READ: MATTHEW 4:18–22

KEY VERSES VV21–22
'Jesus called them, and immediately they left the boat and their father and followed him.'

Imagine your favourite celebrity coming into your room right now and asking whether they could hang out with you for a while – you'd probably say yes, right? What if that celebrity then told you that hanging out might have a bit of a cost attached? That you weren't going to be able to go on social media for a while, that you won't have home-comforts, or that your life might start to look very different from how it looked before. Would you still say yes?

Being a disciple has a cost. It had a cost for the guys in this Bible passage – they had to leave the life they were so comfortable with and follow Jesus into the unknown. But they chose Him over their comfort. Are we prepared to weigh up the cost of being a disciple, knowing that our lives may never be the same as a result?

You might have some idea of what your future path looks like. It's great to have a focus and nurture personal dreams, whatever they might be. But how could you use those dreams for God? Remember, He will be with you every step of the way so you will never be on your own.

Discipleship Tip: Following Jesus means just that: following Him wherever He leads you – but it will definitely be the right path.

Think

If Jesus asked you to alter your life plans in order to do something for Him, would you say yes?

Truth

READ: JOHN 8:31–26

KEY VERSE V32
'Then you will know the truth, and the truth will set you free.'

Fake news is everywhere. It's deliberate disinformation spread through the media or online. The end result is that it is difficult to know what is true or who to believe.

Many people are searching for truth. They think they know where it is but can't quite locate it. Most world-views, religions and even secular views point elsewhere for the truth to be found. This could be Mohammed pointing to Allah, Buddhism pointing to the self or atheism pointing towards science or self-gratification. Jesus is the only character in history bold enough to point to Himself as being the truth. He said: 'I am the way and the truth and the life' (John 14:6). With Jesus, the search is over, the reason for living is found. The massive questions of life are answered with the truth. Choosing to believe that Jesus is the truth is what we call faith, and it's one of the most important parts of being a disciple.

Discipleship Tip: Remember that discipleship is more about faith than feelings. Faith is choosing to believe what's true, and we can choose to believe that Jesus is the way, the truth and the life regardless of how we are feeling.

 ## *Pray*
Lord God, thank You that in You we have truth, that the answers to life's questions can be found in Jesus. Help us to have faith in You by choosing to believe what is really true. Amen.

Time to listen

READ: JOHN 16:12–15

KEY VERSE V13
'But when he, the Spirit of truth, comes, he will guide you into all the truth.'

Jesus, in His time on earth, taught us a lot about what it means to be a disciple and we've studied many of these things over the last few months. Reading the Bible and thinking about His wise words are really important. But it's also really important to know that we have a guide with us who can lead us in the ways of discipleship.

Listening to the Holy Spirit is one of the key disciplines of being a disciple, because it's learning to be in tune with God's presence on earth.

We are often so busy that we don't give time to listen to the voice of God. We are so keen with the results of being a disciple but not keen to do the whole process, because we know that sometimes keeping in tune with the Spirit can be time consuming and tough. Making time to listen and be guided by God can be the last thing we want to do with our days when TV, social networks, friends and gaming beckon us. However, discipline comes from the word 'disciple'. We might not like the idea of discipline but, just like focused athletes, it is what makes us stronger in our faith.

Discipleship Tip: If you want to be a true follower of Jesus, you need to listen and plug into the Holy Spirit, even when it seems tough to do so.

 ## *Think*

Are you giving the Holy Spirit enough time and space to guide you today?

Stay focused

READ: PHILIPPIANS 3:12–14

KEY VERSES VV13–14
'straining towards what is ahead, I press on towards the goal to win the prize for which God has called me heavenwards'

As 2020 comes to an end, there is one final question on the subject of discipleship: where are *you* heading? Paul is writing these words in the book of Philippians, one of the last letters he wrote before being killed for what – and who – he believed in.

Imagine you are running a race at a school's sports day. You and all the other competitors line up at the start, ready to run down the track; the whistle is blown and you're off! You burst into the lead, running with all your heart. You can see the finish line, but wanting to see how you're doing, you look back. Big mistake! In that split second, your lack of focus and concentration means that you have been overtaken by another runner. You finish in third place. Sad times – so near, yet so far.

Let's remember to stay focused on what God is asking us to do as His disciples.

Discipleship Tip: Forget the past and press on to the heavenly prize. Don't look back – you are a new creation. Don't keep trying to see how others are doing – stay in your own lane and keep your eyes on Jesus!

➕ *Challenge*

In 2021, let's make a resolution to not let anything distract us from the goal of following Jesus.